The Diary of a Georgian Shopkeeper

Halland House at the time of the diary:
from T. W. Horsfield, *History, Antiquities, and Topography of the County of Sussex*, 1835

THOMAS TURNER

The Diary of a
Georgian Shopkeeper

A selection by
R. W. BLENCOWE and M. A. LOWER

With a preface by
FLORENCE MARIS TURNER

Second Edition

Edited with a new introduction by
G. H. JENNINGS

Oxford   New York   Toronto   Melbourne
OXFORD UNIVERSITY PRESS
1979

Oxford University Press, Walton Street, Oxford OX2 6DP

OXFORD   LONDON   GLASGOW
NEW YORK   TORONTO   MELBOURNE   WELLINGTON
KUALA LUMPUR   SINGAPORE   JAKARTA   HONG KONG   TOKYO
DELHI   BOMBAY   CALCUTTA   MADRAS   KARACHI
NAIROBI   DAR ES SALAAM   CAPE TOWN

Introduction © *G. H. Jennings 1979*

*First edition in book form published 1925 by John Lane The Bodley Head
Limited as* The Diary of Thomas Turner of East Hoathly (1754–1765)

*Second edition first published as an Oxford University Press paperback
and simultaneously in a hardback edition edited with a new introduction
by G. H. Jennings 1979 at the suggestion of Anne Wilkinson*

British Library Cataloguing in Publication Data
Turner, Thomas
  The diary of a Georgian shopkeeper.
  – 2nd ed.
  1. East Hoathly, Eng. – Social life and customs
  I. Title   II. Blencowe, R W
  III. Lower, M A   IV. Jennings, G H
  942.2′51   DA690.E1/   79-40106

ISBN 0-19-211769-9
ISBN 0-19-281283-1 Pbk

*Printed in Great Britain by
Cox & Wyman Ltd, Reading*

Contents

Publisher's Note on the Text

The manuscript of Turner's diary, originally in the possession of his family, now at Yale University, occupies 111 stout memorandum books (there were originally 116, but five are missing, for a reason as yet obscure). The present selection from the diary was made by R. W. Blencowe and M. A. Lower, and published with running commentary and annotations under the title 'Extracts from the Diary of a Sussex Tradesman, A Hundred Years Ago' in *Sussex Archaeological Collections* 11 (1859), 179–220. It was reissued in book form, without the commentary and many of the notes, by John Lane The Bodley Head Limited in 1925, with an Introduction by J. B. Priestley, the present Preface by Florence Maris Turner (Mrs Charles Lamb), great-great-granddaughter of the diarist, and the Appendix giving the diarist's notes on his family history. Florence Maris Turner was styled 'Editor' in this reissue, and she did not make it clear that she reproduced Blencowe and Lower's selection without subtraction, addition or rearrangement, and included a number of their footnotes, slightly modified. There is no evidence that she consulted the original diary at all: on the contrary, she made no attempt to place the entries in their proper order, or to indicate where the beginning of an entry had been omitted (Blencowe and Lower have clearly not given their extracts in exclusively chronological order, and they sometimes begin a new extract without giving its date: in these cases Florence Turner allows the new extract to follow the previous one without a break, as if the two belonged to the same date).

The editor of the present, revised edition, Dr G. H. Jennings, has given Blencowe and Lower their due, and has attempted, as far as is possible without reference to the original diary, to place the entries in chronological order.[1] But it is certain that some further rearrangement remains to be done.[2] Where Blencowe and Lower begin an extract from a new entry without giving a date, an asterisk has been printed to mark the discontinuity.

It is evident from a comparison of the diary with the Appendix that Blencowe and Lower to some degree modernised Turner's punctuation, and perhaps his spelling too. Further adjustments of this kind, some unintentional, were made in the 1925 edition. The present edition follows Blencowe and Lower, and whole lines accidentally omitted in the 1925 edition have been reinstated.

Footnotes followed by 'B. and L.' are derived, more or less closely, from Blencowe and Lower's commentary or notes. Other annotations, apart from one by Florence Turner, marked 'F.M.T.', are by Dr Jennings.

1979

[1] The publishers would like to take this opportunity of thanking Dr Jennings for his prodigious labours on the diary, undertaken under severe pressure of time. His intimate knowledge of Sussex, and his wide historical learning generally, have enabled him to make this edition a great improvement on its predecessor. It was his own article in *Country Life* (12 October 1978, pp. 1118 and 1120), 'Diary of a Georgian Shopkeeper', which stimulated this reissue, and gave it its title.

[2] If interest in the present edition of the diary is as strong as the publishers anticipate, it is proposed to consult the original diary with a view to improving and possibly expanding this selection when it is reprinted.

Introduction

G. H. JENNINGS

This selection[1] of extracts from the intimate diary of
Thomas Turner, shopkeeper and general dealer of
East Hoathly in Sussex, tells in random but graphic
manner a story of the lives of our South Country ancestors. It is largely set in the shadow of the Seven
Years' War, but the diarist's own story stands out
from his pages with almost confessional clarity.
Readers will agree with his descendant, Mrs Charles
Lamb, in her excellent preface, that his account needs
no elaboration. My chief aim is to provide more con-
text for his entries.

Why did Turner write this diary and why did he
discontinue it? Living in the village of the Prime
Minister (who at that time was styled 'First Lord of
the Treasury') and in close contact with national
events, he may have felt the need to chronicle them.
This he did in clear handwriting; he is direct and out-
spoken with none of the secrecy of Pepys: 'Let me
now describe my uneasy situation,' he writes, con-
scious of the fact that he may have a reader. Certainly
he regards himself as an educated man (13 August
1764), and as former village schoolmaster is ready to
instruct. He is also a 'rustic moralist', but much of his
moralising is aimed at himself. He is essentially a

[1] By R. W. Blencowe and M. A. Lower: see Publisher's Note
on the Text, p.vii above.

lonely figure among his many drinking acquaintances; he laments their mindless lapses into drunkenness (5 December 1757). But he rejoices when there is good company: 'prodigiously delighted with each other's company and at the same time we went to bed sober' (15 November 1759). His wife is a chronic invalid and they have lost their only child. His diary is both his companion and his memoir. It is a rich mine of information about its period; it contains both farce and deep tragedy. The spelling, particularly after his drinking bouts, is of the 'hit or miss' variety, but the chief humour is unconscious and flows from his moralising and self-exhortation. The farther the reader probes into the diary the more ludicrous becomes it portentous opening entry. And what can we say of a churchwarden who chronicles his rejection of the Sunday offertory plate with: 'Oh may we increase in faith and good works'! Not a hypocrite, we feel, but a man very deficient in humour in times which were far from joyful. It is to be hoped that his uplifting sentiments had some effect in raising his morale, but alas, no consistent benefit is apparent.

The diary ends with his staid account of his second wooing, and the concluding appendix gives full details of his family. He was presumably content with this family life, despite its occasional tragedies, and with it no longer had time or need for his diary. His business also must have increased after the Peace of 1763, for he was a capable and ambitious shopkeeper, and happiest when most busy: 'At home all day, and, thank GOD, extremely busy' (14 August 1758) leads him to reflect on the joys of good trade; while the lack of it produces 'a most prodigious mellancholy time' (15 July 1758).[1]

He was responsible for the supply not only of a large countryside area, but also for the great celebratory feasts of Thomas Pelham, First Duke of Newcastle, at Halland House. The Duke was by turn Prime Minister (1754–6) and Lord Treasurer (1756–61) in Pitt's Government, and the roistering sounds of his banquets shake the foundations of Halland at intervals throughout the diary. So Thomas Turner's shop had to be well provisioned with food and drink as well as stocked for much other business (see Preface). The great Elizabethan House lay in its park behind the village, but after the Duke's death in 1768 it gradually fell into decay; much of his fortune had been spent.

The importance of the Pelhams was at its zenith between 1739 and 1762, when first the younger brother Henry and then Thomas had supreme influence either as Prime Minister or First Lord of the Treasury; but their family power was deep-rooted. The 'Pelham Buckle' on their seal and on many church towers built by them in East Sussex recalled the sword-buckle of the French King captured by Sir

[1] By the beginning of the nineteenth century the diarist's son, Frederick, had impressive trade returns, assessed by Blencowe and Lower at as high as £50,000 annually!

John Pelham at Poitiers in 1356. They had great wealth, and extensive estates between Lewes and Battle. First Pevensey Castle, then Laughton Place (built in 1534) and the great Halland House (built in 1595), were their homes. In 1653 they bought Pelham House (built in 1563) in Lewes for use as a 'winter house' and as a residence during great occasions in Lewes. (It is now Council offices.) They defended the surrounding coastal country against French incursions, and the memorial to Sir Nicholas Pelham in St Michael's, Lewes, recalls a day in 1545:

> What time the French sought to have sackt Sea-Foord
> This Pelham did repel-em back aboord.

Such were the antecedents of the great Duke of Newcastle whom Thomas Turner served during the period of the diary and whose progress through his domains from his coastal Bishopstone manor was marked by ringing of the church bells. He was a generous man who would certainly leave no thirsty ringers behind him. As a politician he was an indecisive leader, but a great party manager; he had vast wealth and his lavish spending in the Halland feasts was an instance of his use of his riches to secure power. 'Mr Pitt does all while the Duke pays all' was Horace Walpole's summary of the strange partnership which brought this country victory in the Seven Years' War (1756–63). Of the Pelham houses Halland and Bishopstone have gone; Stanmer Park ('Stanmore' in the diary) is the headquarters of Sussex

University; and Laughton Place is a lonely moated tower beside the upper tidal waters of Glynde Reach.[1] In the Pelham family vault of Laughton church lie two former Prime Ministers of England, Henry and Thomas Pelham, with more than thirty other members of a family for so long supreme in this countryside. But the family is now elsewhere and for a hundred years the vault has been sealed.

One isolated late entry, recorded by Blencowe and Lower, follows the main diary. On 18 November 1768 the Duke of Newcastle was buried with great splendour at Laughton. The chief mourner, John Pelham Esq., was in the first coach with the officiating clergy: the Bishop of Norwich, Dr Hurdis (the Duke's Chaplain), and the Rev. Thomas Hurdis.[2] All the other coaches were filled by the Duke's servants. His tenants and the parishioners from neighbouring parishes rode two by two to close the procession. The last comment on this event may well come from Thomas Turner: 'But not one of the many noble and gentle guests who, as we have seen, had been so often partakers of his noisy but splendid hospitality,

[1] When the Duke died, without issue, in 1768, he was succeeded by his next of kin Sir Thomas Pelham of Stanmer. This gentleman was 'improving' Stanmer Park and removed the floors and staircases from Halland to assist in this process. Later, bricks were removed from the old house to build up the farm at Halland and the old house was gradually demolished.

[2] Rev. James Hurdis of this Bishopstone family was Professor of Poetry at Oxford at the turn of the eighteenth century.

followed to the grave the remains of the first and last Duke of Newcastle.' It was the end of an epoch.

East Hoathly still has a direct personal link with Thomas Turner, and there are many legible stones in the churchyards of East Hoathly and Framfield to commemorate members of his family. His own small memorial inscribed 'Thomas Turner . . . Draper' lies outside the east end of East Hoathly church; but his house, with its inscribed memorial plaque, is a shop no more.

The road through the village is now a busy one, but the level lands around it still support a mixed agriculture as at the time of the diary. The once sodden soil is now well drained and the scattered farms are accessible. Whyly, the manorial farm of the French family which features so memorably in the pages of the diary, has gone. The present farms tend to be large, and one occupies Halland Park. At the time of the diary there were only a few large farms, and though three-quarters of the seventy-five village families were yeomen leaseholders, their farms were mostly small; the other cottagers (over a hundred people) worked as labourers or servants. There were a number of bad harvests at the time of the diary; its pages reveal destitution in many families (26 September and 7 December 1763). This was aggravated by the increasing enclosure of common land and by the aggregation of smaller into larger estates. Corn prices were kept up by the machinations of middlemen ('ingrossors', 23 March 1758), and by the War's

effect on taxation of land, houses, windows and
malt. The Rector, Rev. Thomas Porter, is forced to
demolish a farmhouse on his land and finds a golden
'Jacobus' and silver coins. Like the Duke, he has hop-
fields, but most of the crops and stock carried by the
farms in the district were the traditional ones: every
species of grain was grown at East Hoathly and
Chiddingly, as well as hops; at Laughton they grew
peas, beans, cabbage, onions and leeks, and all
grains except barley. Salads, potatoes, parsnips and
carrots were also cultivated. The stock included
cattle, sheep, pigs and poultry; bees were kept
(4 October 1758). A survey of the two dozen meals[1]
listed in this selection from the diary confirms this
impression, besides showing the enduring popularity
of sausages, 'rasures' of bacon, and plum-pudding on
Christmas Day! Oxen were used to draw the ploughs
and wagons across the heavy land, and horses had to
be used for travel except when the paths dried out in
summer. Then the mountebanks and travelling
tradesmen took to the roads: fishermen, merchants
with wagon-loads of goods (6 July 1764), masons,
bricklayers, hop-pickers etc. East Hoathly had not
only its shop and two alehouses (Jones's and Pralls's),
but also a butcher, shoemaker, chandler, blacksmith
and carpenter-wheelwright; as well as a weaver and a
barber.

[1] Not surprisingly there is much more mention (42 times) of
drink (beer, wine, gin, brandy and punch—including 'bumbo')
than of food in the selected diary.

The high Excise Duty and the accessibility of this area of Sussex from the sea made smuggling a recognized way of life.[1] The Custom-house was at Newhaven (15 June 1764), but at Pevensey Bay[2] or nearby Cuckmere Haven, a dozen miles south of East Hoathly, were good quiet beaches where the smugglers of the Alfriston area could land their contraband French brandy (24 November 1763). It was then sent to the Forest Ridge (Mayfield, Burwash, Robertsbridge etc.) and so towards London through a chain of 'receiving' cottages. Dark nights were used for this business, as Horace Walpole learnt to his cost. Finding travel difficult, he and his friend decided to put up at the Robertsbridge Inn, but found all the beds occupied by smugglers who were posing as 'mountybanks'. So they pushed on to Battle, which was full of excisemen who had just shot a smuggler. Feeling very insecure, they took 'links and lanthorns' and dragged their way through the mud to their destination at Hurstmonceux. Mountebanks were frequent summer travellers in Sussex, and the diary describes one (9 July 1760). They were entertaining charlatans who fiddled, tumbled and juggled before selling their packets of a quack powder mixture, 'Universal Hodg-Podg', to simple-minded country folk.

[1] Smuggled goods included spirits, tea, silks, tobacco, coffee, cocoa and chocolate.

[2] In 1744 such a large gang of smugglers landed from the Bay that they were mistaken for the French and the Duke of Newcastle hastened to repel the 'invasion'!

The popularity of such quacks is attributable to the appalling standards of health and treatment at the time. The prescriptions of the parish surgeon (mostly purges and placebos) were futile in face of such endemic diseases as smallpox, typhoid, diptheria, tuberculosis, malaria (ague) and scarlet fever, to name but a few. These spread rapidly because of overcrowding, lack of sanitation, and malnutrition. Even pneumonia and appendicitis, imperfectly understood, were usually fatal. Death recurs throughout the diary, but mortality was far higher in London where it much exceeded the birthrate. That great eighteenth-century menace, drink, caused death both directly, as in Mr French Snr, whose liver is shrivelled by vast consumption of gin (17 September 1763), and also indirectly, by deflecting money from food purchase. Malnutrition, exposure to cold (11 January 1764), and a large infant population facilitated the spread of infections. The popular treatment of 'inoculation' with a small live smallpox dose, introduced by Lady Mary Wortley Montagu from Turkey in 1718, is in the diary associated with two deaths, including a Turner infant (Appendix, p. 84). It was a hazardous treatment at a time when all life was precarious, particularly for the young. The fate of Mary Shoosmith (aged 16), of a good Laughton family and working as maid at the Rectory, illustrates the extent of such hazards (12 December 1757).

Turner himself, though at times contemplating the

possibility of dying when in liquor (21 February 1761), is evidently a man of robust constitution. He does not seem to be addicted to neat gin (a more urban vice), but brandy punch (especially the spiced cold form, 'bumbo') often causes him to fall from grace. His unfortunate wife's health is not equal to the strain of the bacchanalia in Lent 1758, and soon afterwards her long illness begins. The part played by the Rector at this season is so remarkable that I merely commend the reader to notice how easily the whole matter sits on his conscience. Not so with Turner; as always, drink fills him with remorse and guilt, and not until ten days later (17 March 1758) does he dare to exclaim: 'Now, I hope all revelling for this season is over'! But the hope is vain; 'that hateful vice of drunkenness—a crime almost productive of all other vices' pursues him through the diary. Nor does he spare the Duke on his 'Publick Days' for countenancing 'levity, drunkenness, and all sorts of immorality' (Sunday, 5 August 1759). A slight exaggeration, perhaps, but did not Archbishop Tillotson charge men with the duty of setting a good example—especially with villagers, including beggars, present among their betters?[1]

The Church of the time reflected the tolerant easygoing Archbishop's views in precept if not in practice. Enthusiasm for religion could be left to the Methodists; otherwise it was rather bad form.

The Hoathly Rector, Rev. Thomas Porter, A.M.,

[1] For Tillotson see p. 14, note 1.

seems to have been a capable preacher, but Sunday services were not consistently held at his church, and even then a number were taken by neighbouring curates. Pluralism was rife at the time and 'an idle, lazy way of preaching' is remarked. Curates were paid about £40 a year and many were 'perpetual'; not surprising, then, that the poor Laughton curate was both in debt and in drink on 25 November 1763. Mr Porter lasted in his comfortable living till 1795. Turner was Churchwarden and Vestry Overseer; in the latter capacity he was responsible for preventing Sunday drinking in the alehouses.[1] So he should have avoided the 'horrors' of being drunk in Jones's on Sunday 28 March 1756. Perhaps that memory was responsible for his subsequent leniency to the barber and other possible breakers of the Sabbath. Certainly he discovers no 'disorderly fellows' in the alehouses 'proper to send' to sea (Sunday 2 April 1758).

The Overseer was the chief executive officer, with two assistants, 'Electioners'; this trio at East Hoathly were Messrs Turner, Hope and Vine. The vestries, set up during the reign of Elizabeth I, dealt with all matters of parish administration, including that of the Poor Law. They had increased powers in the eighteenth century when central government had

---

[1] The Overseer was also responsible for upkeep of 'roads' and settling trade disputes. Cf. 4 October 1758, 30 June 1764 and 20 February 1765. The post seems to have been unpaid in Turner's time; as also those of the Electioners (surveyors). There was no legalised Overseer's pay until 1819.

devolved much local power. Horace Walpole commented: 'I have sometimes thought that a Squire and Vestry were a King and Republic in miniature.' The 'King' of East Hoathly was the Duke, and he did not exercise tyranny, as implied by Walpole, being so much involved in central government. Nor was the Vestry of East Hoathly very effective. Its meetings were held in John Jones's alehouse where quarrelling and 'vollies' of 'vile oaths' often nullified all discussion. Swearing is regularly condemned by Turner, and it was so free that Mr Porter was constrained to cease from merriment and preach against it (5 March 1758). Failure to declare liabilities for Poor Rate and other taxes is stigmatised by the diarist as 'robbing . . . of the community' (24 March 1763). But two positive actions are recorded; the first is the sending of constables ('Headboroughs' Hooke and Hudson) to apprehend a father who has long deserted his family. The second is the calculated shedding of a liability by buying an awkward couple a 'settlement' in the next parish (Waldron). Another record shows the constables being sent to arrest the 'putative father' of an unborn village infant. Such illegitimate children were 'on the parish' if the father was not made responsible. This problem explains to some extent Turner's abhorrence of the restrictive Marriage Act,[1] and the reason he subscribed for the clergy who

[1] The Marriage Act forbade girls under the age of 21 to marry; Hardwicke's Act (1753) made Anglican clergy responsible for all marriages.

were in Horsham Gaol for marrying 'under-age' girls (11 January 1758). His attitude, partly the official one of an overseer, is also coloured by compassion. The account (8 March 1760) of the night suicide of young Lucy Mott ('there is . . . the greatest reason imaginable to think that she was pregnant') recalls in all its pathetic detail the Wessex of Thomas Hardy.

Another terrible tragedy, in July 1757 (recorded by Blencowe and Lower but omitted by Florence Maris Turner) is detailed in the full diary. Turner gives a lengthy account of the callous murder of an unfortunate village girl in a wood at night. Her seducer poisons her with arsenic and when she reaches home watches her death agonies till she is silent. The case concerned one of the principal men in the village and he was later acquitted at Lewes after an inquest which seems to have been a travesty of justice.

Details of the Relief which Turner arranged for the parish can be seen from his bills of the time. These include provision of food, fuel and clothing for the poor, while the old, sick or destitute were boarded out with other families at five shillings a week. The bill for one year of Nathaniel Paine, parish surgeon, amounted to £26 5s. 6d. for provision of many simple medicines and salves, and for cutting 'an issue'. The undertaker (Turner) charged twelve shillings each for four pauper's coffins. The Pelham Charity (21 December 1759) amounted to £9 annually and that of Samuel Atkins (died 1742) to £4 a year.

that of Samuel Atkins (died 1742) to £4 a year.

The plight of the young, quite apart from their health, was very grievous. There were almost no facilities for education. Schools such as Thomas Turner is running for 3*d*. a week when the diary opens were at best places for learning a little of the three Rs. At Mayfield, a larger place, there was a teacher, Walter Gale, employed by the Parish until he was sacked for negligence.[1] The diary of this erratic contemporary of Turner records a Sunday visit to East Hoathly when the Rector preached on the text 'Take no thought, saying "What shall we eat and what shall we drink?" ' etc. Gale's response was to cross the road to Jones's after the service for two pints of 'twopenny' (strong beer at twopence a pint); luckily no overseer was in sight!

Some old towns had their Grammar Schools where 'little Latin and less Greek' were taught. Such were the Free Grammar School at Steyning with fifty pupils and that at South Malling (Lewes) where another diarist, John Evelyn, attended. Sunday Schools were not started until 1780, and most children had no formal education. At the age of seven most East Hoathly children went out as servants or to help on the land; this also applied to the unwanted

[1] 'Old Kent', one of the Mayfield elders, was wont to menace him regularly at school, shouting: 'The greater the scholler, the greater the rogue!' Gale's sister lived at Laughton. He must have been a considerable 'scholler' since Mr Porter employed him to transcribe Latin translations of Greek verse back into Greek Sapphics.

ones who survived 'nurse' or workhouse. Some boys were apprenticed in trade, as was Moses Turner to a tailor in Lewes, and a fee of £5 or so was paid to the master. Unwanted children went for less, and always the term was to the age of twenty-one. It was a system wide open to brutality, particularly in towns or at sea. Children could help their parents, but these were sometimes amongst the harshest employers. Girls usually went out as servants ('childmaids'), and those from good families seem to have gone to the better homes; Mary Shoosmith at the Rectory came of a family who provided churchwardens at Laughton for over two hundred years. Turner's second wife, Molly Hicks, was servant to a Lewes gentleman and the last entry in the diary suggests that her father, a yeoman farmer of Chiddingly, was quite affluent. Thomas Turner had three servants, two boys and a girl; he seems to have been an indulgent master, the boys growing very cheeky as time goes on (28 March 1762). Horace Walpole, influenced no doubt by Tillotson, went to church to set an example to his servants, saying: 'A good moral sermon may instruct and benefit them.' Turner's Christmas Day in 1757 shows that he followed a similar practice, which recurs throughout the book.

The Seven Years' War, as has already been remarked, occasioned much hardship and anxiety in the Sussex countryside, but it did give an extra dimension to life, particularly in the great Minister's village. There is strong reaction to all national events

by the diarist, who is the Duke's caterer. First comes
an outburst of intense patriotic grief when Byng
abandons Minorca (18 July 1756), to be followed by
admiration of 12,000 of Pitt's newly mobilised
troops at Church Parade on Cox Heath (15 August
1756). Then Prince Ferdinand of Brunswick, with
our Prussian allies, beats the French at Crefeld (29
June 1758) and sets the bells ringing; bonfires and
feasting at Halland soon followed. This was the pat-
tern after all the great victories of the War except
when Wolfe was killed, and then rejoicing gave way
to a Thanksgiving Prayer in the churches (28 October
1759). The diarist regularly attended the victory
feasts at Halland, ostensibly so as not to 'disoblige'
Mr Coates, the Duke's agent and the shop's best
customer, but he seems to have entered into the usual
practice of 'drinking many loyall healths' and in consequence 'came home very much in liquor' leaving
'not one sober person in company'. The scene is
repeated in celebration of the fall of Louisbourg (23
August 1758) and after Prince Ferdinand's great victory at Minden (5 August 1759). News travelled
slowly and the celebrations followed more distant
events at a few weeks' interval. There were scares of
invasion, for the French were massing troops across
the channel, and a false report of a landing is in the
entry for 7 July 1759; this was soon to be cancelled
by news of Rodney's bombardment of Le Havre. But
the crowning news is that of Admiral Hawke's won-
derful victory of Quiberon Bay on 20 November

1759, where, amid rocks and shoals and despite fierce winter storms, he smashed the French invasion fleet. The muddy roads kept the news from Halland till 8 December, but then rejoicing knew no bounds; after the celebrations the diarist is nearly 'scuppered' in the Rector's wood! But he gets home early on that winter morning thanking Divine Providence for his preservation.

Hawke and Boscawen had also severed French sea routes and next year the French armies were driven from India by Eyre Coote, and out of Canada by Amherst. Thomas missed the Halland celebrations for the conquest of Canada (7 October 1760) because his wife Peggy was 'prodigiously ill'. The War was drawing to a close, and George II, much lamented in the diary, died later that October. His son replaced Pitt with Bute; there is a mere Thanksgiving Prayer for the capture of Martinique (4 April 1762), but no one in East Hoathly observed the official rejoicings on 5 May 1763 for what they generally regarded as an 'inglorious' peace. (We ceded many conquests and deserted our Prussian allies in the Treaty of Paris, at a time when France was almost on her knees.)

Although Pitt's power was waning in 1761 the diary shows that his partner, Newcastle, still had his hands firmly on the reins. On 7 April 1761 the diarist is in a great flurry while the Duke entertains five hundred local people before they attend him to Lewes for the county elections. The result, as usual in boroughs (between 6 and 12 'pocket' boroughs at different times) under the Duke's influence, is a foregone conclusion—'no opposition'.

Lewes featured as an Assize town every year in August, and the neighbourhood was then briefly *en fête*. For at least two days a Race Meeting was held on the Downs under the Duke's stewardship, with the King's Plate (£100) as chief prize. There was an evening ball in Lewes on King's Plate Day ('an extreme pretty sight', 12 August 1757) and the usual 'publick day' at Halland for the Judges preceded the week. The Race-course, an attractive open place on the Downs beside the battlefield of Lewes where Simon de Montfort defeated Henry III in 1264, was the scene of a great deal of drinking and betting.

A rapid glance through the diary shows the many eighteenth-century pastimes: cards, horse racing, human racing, and especially the vile tavern cock-fighting, were disfigured by drink and gaming. Cricket, patronised by the upper class, was a better-ordered game. Eleven-a-side matches at Mayfield, watched by Walter Gale, and at East Hoathly, where Turner participated, seem quite decorous. Brighton ('Brighthelmstone near Lewes' at the outset of the diary) was to develop, not only into a health resort, but also into a cradle of cricket. Nyren's Hambledon Club in Hampshire, predecessor of the M.C.C., was soon being watched by large gatherings on Broad-Halfpenny Down. Players came from far and wide, and early summer mornings at Northchapel (West Sussex) could reveal a great hitter, Noah Mann, the local innkeeper, setting out on his twenty-mile ride to Hambledon. The Laws of the ancient game of cricket were formulated in 1744, and amongst its early patrons was the 3rd Duke of Dorset, a keen player. His father, Lord John Sackville, early sounded the democratic note in cricket by playing under the captaincy of the Knole gardener!

This new edition of Turner's diary should make many friends for a man who rarely left his small country arena. Its account of eighteenth-century foibles and follies, joys and sorrows, could serve as jottings for a sequel to *Tom Jones*. We can also glimpse the passing seasons: very thick ice one winter; a very wet July; a cataclysmic summer storm; a very early spring in 1759; and the glorious Sussex Maytimes. Turner is equally interested in the beautiful new Palladian mansion at Mereworth and the fine 'Gothic' Abbey at Battle—though his figures of English dead in that battle are rather horrific! He is a keen if indiscriminate reader, on whose shelves Sherlock's *On Death* rubs shoulders with Wilkes's *On Liberty*. He marvels at Hawksbee's friction electricity and Graham's clockwork 'microcosm' (i.e. orrery or model planetarium). Turner has left us in his debt, not only for his comments from the wings on the Seven Years' War, but also for this picturesque presentation of his own very personal microcosm.

Northchapel, Petworth

Preface

FLORENCE MARIS TURNER

At the outset sincere thanks must be given to the Sussex Archaeological Society for permission to make full use of the transcription of Thomas Turner's Diary published in vol. 11 of the *Sussex Archaeological Collections* in 1859 with extensive comments and notes by the Editors R. W. Blencowe, Esq., M.A., and M. A. Lower, Esq., M.A., F.S.A.

Since the publication many articles with copious quotations have appeared from time to time. Charles Dickens contributed one to *All the Year Round*; *Glimpses of our Sussex Ancestors* by Charles Fleet, published in 1882, contains twenty-one pages of a most interesting character with reference to it; and in 1923 Arthur Ponsonby, in his *English Diaries from the Sixteenth to Twentieth Century*, devotes a chapter of sympathetic appreciation to the old Diarist.

It is not a little interesting to compare the views of Thomas Turner's successive critics: views which were naturally dependent on a focus which the passing of years is for ever changing.

If anything can be said to speak for itself surely a diary must come under that heading, yet it is hoped that a few notes may not be out of place.

Thomas Turner was born in the third year of George II's reign, 1729, at Groombridge, Kent. 'Thomas, son of John Turner and his wife', so runs the entry of his christening in the parish register. His pedigree is uncertain, but there is no doubt as to his exceptional mental ability. He is believed to be descended from the Old Sussex County Family the Turners of Tablehurst, East Grinstead. That he owned a painting of the Turner coat of arms is very strong evidence, and an inherent refinement is suggested by his love of fine literature, and the fact that, in spite of the village shop, he moved on terms of equality and intimacy with the local gentlefolk. An exception, when on the non-arrival of some goods, Mrs Porter, the vicar's wife, 'treated me with as much imperious and scornful usage as if she had been, what I think she is, more of a Turk and an Infidel than a Christian and I an abject slave', points not so much to Turner's lack of breeding as to Mrs Porter's.

He commenced his diary in 1754, in which year he is found to be living in East Hoathly, Sussex, following the calling of schoolmaster. The duties were probably uncongenial, they were certainly unremunerative, for at that time 3d. a week was paid for tuition. It is not surprising that Thomas Turner soon found a far more satisfactory outlet for his stupendous energy in trade, and, taking a shop in the village, he started business as a general dealer. To describe him as general dealer is not to overstate the case. He was grocer, draper, haberdasher, hatter, clothier, druggist, ironmonger, stationer, glover, undertaker, besides dealing in the hop and wheat crops of the county. In his spare moments he officiated as arbitrator in trade and other disputes, and kept a diary.

He has often been compared with Samuel Pepys, and the two men had much in common. Pepys had the advantage of living in London and during times for which 'stirring' is a mild word. It speaks volumes for Turner's personality that he could invest with such absorbing interest the chronicle of daily life in a remote Sussex village.

Both Thomas Turner and his illustrious predecessor, in giving to posterity a most vivid picture of their age, gave at the same time a no less vivid picture of themselves; yet in neither case is there any of that pronounced egotism and morbid introspection which pervades so many diaries. The nearest approach to it lies in Turner's remorse for his constant lapses from sobriety, and his good resolutions which, it must be confessed, usually melt away before the ink is dry. In fairness it must be said that the Diarist at least felt some compunction at his own shortcomings, but there seem to have been no such signs of grace on the part of Mr Porter, the Vicar of the parish, who in these scandalous exhibitions figures not merely as participator but ringleader. Turner's excuses are not unreasonable: 'If I goe I must drink just as they please or otherwise I shall be called a poor singular fellow. If I stay at home I shall be stigmatized with the name of being a poor, proud, ill-natured wretch and perhaps disoblige Mr Coates' (Duke of Newcastle's Agent). As Arthur Ponsonby observes in *English*

PREFACE

Diaries from the Sixteenth to Twentieth Century:
'Turner always goes though he knows what the result will be.' Some lenient critic of life has said that
vices are only virtues carried to excess; the charitably
minded will admit that it was excess of hospitality
and good fellowship which so often reduced our
Diarist to the condition he describes as 'being far
from bad company'.

Thomas Turner married twice. His first wife,
Peggy Slater, dies after being 'most prodigious bad'.
The disease is not stated, but seeing she took an active part in the amazing orgies that went on, her constitution, even if normally sound, must have been
severely tried. His second wife is one Molly Hicks,
daughter of a Yeoman farmer, whom he marries in
1765, and there the diary ends. As an historical account of English village life at the time it is probably
without parallel; and not least among the many
reasons for its abiding interest are the wholesome
sanity, the frailty and the warm, glowing humanity
of the old Sussex Diarist.

The strong personality manifest in, and between,
so many of the lines he penned, is not an unlovable
one even if his footprints on the sands of Time are so
often devious and erratic.

To those who are making his acquaintance for the
first time, and without regret, this volume is
dedicated.

The Diary

1754

Sunday, Feb. 8, 1754.—As I by experience find how much more conducive it is to my health, as well as pleasantness and serenity to my mind, to live in a low, moderate rate of diet, and as I know I shall never be able to comply therewith in so strickt a manner as I should chuse, by the unstable and over-easyness of my temper, I think it therefore fit to draw up Rules of proper Regimen, which I do in the manner and form following, which I hope I shall always have the strictest regard to follow, as I think they are not inconsistent with either religion or morality . . .

If I am at home, or in company abroad, I will never drink more than four glasses of strong beer: one to toast the King's health, the second to the Royal Family, the third to all friends, and the fourth to the pleasure of the company. If there is either wine or punch, never upon any terms or perswasion to drink more than eight glasses, each glass to hold no more than half a quarter of a pint.

June 26, 1754.—This day made an end of instructing Miss Day. Read part of the *Spectator*; prodigiously admire the beautys pointed out in the eighth book of Milton's *Paradise Lost*, by the *Spectator's* criticism wherein is beautifully expressed Adam's conference with the Almighty, and likewise his distress on losing sight of the phantom in his dream, and his joy in finding it a real creature when awake.

*

Clarissa Harlow, I look upon as a very well-wrote thing, tho' it must be allowed it is too prolix. The author keeps up the character of every person in all places; and as to the maner of its ending, I like it better than if it had terminated in more happy consequences.[1]

*

My wife read to me that moving scene of the funeral of Miss Clarissa Harlow. Oh, may the Supreme Being give me grace to lead my life in such a manner as my exit may in some measure be like that divine creature's.

July 27.—At home all day. Read part of Boyle's *Lectures*, and Smart's *Poem on Eternity and Immensity*.

Sunday, Aug. 11.—This day, the public day at Halland, the two judges cames from Lewes, and dined there. There was in the whole but a small company. I came home a little past nine, with several of the parishioners, a little matter enlivened by liquor, but no wayes drunk. Not at church all day. My wife went down to Halland to see the turtle.

---

[1] The exact dates of this and the next entry are uncertain, but they suggest that the Turners were reading *Clarissa Harlow* together through much of July 1754.

Monday, 11th.[1]—This day the assizes at Lewes, and only one prisoner.

1755

March 13, 1755.—I went to Mr. Millar's at Burg Hill. Mr. Millar promised me his son should come to me to school. I received of him 18*d.* due to Mr. Tomsett, for schooling Henry.

June 20.—This day being my birthday,[2] I treated my scholars with about five quarts of strong beer, and had an issue cut in my leg.

Fryday, 22nd.—In the evening I read part of the fourth volume of the *Tatler*; the oftener I read it the better I like it. I think I never found the vice of drinking so well exploded in my life, as in one of the numbers.

30th.—This morn my wife and I had words about her going to Lewes to-morrow; Oh, what happiness must there be in the married state, when there is a sincere regard on both sides, and each partie truly satisfied with each other's merits! But it is impossible for tongue or pen to express the uneasiness that attends the contrary.

*

Oh, was marriage ever designed to make mankind unhappy? No, unless by their own choise it's made so by both parties being not satisfied with each other's

[1] An error for 12 August.
[2] In the Appendix the birth date is stated as 9 June (O.S.); the 'lost eleven days' when the N.S. was adopted at the end of 1752 account for the change to 20 June.

merit. But sure this cannot be my own affair, for I married, if I know my own mind, intirely to make my wife and self happy; to live in a course of virtue and religion, and to be a mutual help to each other. Oh! what am I going to say! I have almost made as it were, a resolution to make a sepperation by settling my affairs and parting in friendship. But is this what I married for? How are my views frustrated from the prospect of an happy and quiet life, to the enjoyment of one that is quite the opposite! Oh! were I endued with the patience of Socrates, then might I be happy; but as I am not, I must pacify myself with the cheerful reflection that I have done my utmost to render our union happy, good, and comfortable to ourselves and progeny.

1756

Sunday, March 21.—I was at home all day, but not at church. Oh fye! No just reason for not being there.

Sunday, 28th.—I went down to Jones, where we drank one bowl of punch and two muggs of bumboo; and I came home again in liquor. Oh! with what horrors does it fill my heart, to think I should be guilty of doing so, and on a Sunday too! Let me once more endeavour never, no never to be guilty of the same again.

April 10.—I carried down to Mr. Porter's some shagg, for a pair of breeches for Mr. Porter.

April 19, 1756.—I went down to the vestry, there

being a public vestry at Jones's to chuse new officers; those chosen for the years 1756–7, was Jo. Fuller, churchwarden; John Vine, electioner;[1] myself, overseer; Edward Hope, electioner.

April 21.—I went to the audit, and came home drunk; but I think never to exceed the bounds of moderation more.

Sunday, 25th.—As soon as prayers were ended, Mr. French and I went and searched the public houses. At Francis Turner's we found a man and his wife; they seemed to be very sober sort of people, and not a-drinking, so we did not meddle with them.

28th.—I read several numbers of the *Freeholder*, which I think is a proper book for any person at this critical juncture of affairs. Read Homer's *Odysseyes*. I think the character which Menelaus gives Telemachus of Ulisses, when he is a speaking of his warlike virtues, in the 4th Book, is very good. Read the 13th Book, after supper; I think the soliloquy which Ulysses makes when he finds the Phoenicians have in his sleep left him on his native shore of Ithaca, with all his treasure, contains a very good lesson of morality.

May 3, 1756.—Saw, in the Lewes paper of this day that on Saturday last there was several expolsions heard in the bowels of the earth, like an earthquake, in the parishes of Waldron and

---

[1] Electioner was the assistant and deputy of the overseer in case of absence or sickness. B. and L.

Hellingly.[1]

May 15, 1756.—This day I resigned up my school to Francis Elless.

Friday, May 20.[2]—This day I went to Mr. Porter's to inform them that the livery lace was not come, when I think Mrs. Porter[3] treated me with as much imperious and scornful usage as if she had been what I think she is, more of a Turk and Infidel, than a Christian, and I an abject slave.

July 9.—Mr. French cal'd me to go to Laughton with him, in order to see a funerall there—to wit, the Hon. Lady Frances, Dowager of Castlecomers, sister to his Grace the Duke of Newcastle. She was brought to Halland about eleven o'clock, but not taken out of the hearse, and was intered in their family vault at Laughton, about thirty minutes past one, in the sixty-ninth year of her age. The pall was supported by the Hon. Col. Pelham, Sir Francis Poole, —Campion, Esq., T. Pelham, Esq., John Pelham, Esq., and Henry Pelham. The funeral service was read by the Bishop of Chichester. There were three mourning coaches, Mr. Pelham's, and Colonel Pelham's, and the Bishop's.

July 18.—I this day heard of the lost of Fort St.

[1] The earthquake which destroyed Lisbon and was felt in this country. For months afterwards a sort of panic on the subject of earthquakes prevailed. B. and L.

[2] In 1756 it was 21 May that fell on a Friday.

[3] Mrs Porter was daughter and co-heiress of a wealthy Yorkshire gentleman.

Philip, and the whole island of Minarco [Minorca],[1]
after being possessed by the English nation forty-
seven years, and after being defended ten weeks and
one day, by that truly brave and heroick man,
General Blakeney, and at last was obliged to surrender for want of provision and ammunition. No man,
I think, can deserve a brighter caracter in the annals
of fame than this. But, Oh! he was, as one may justly
say, abandoned by his country, who never sent him
any succours. Never did the English nation suffer a
greater blot. Oh, my country! my country! oh,
Albian, Albian! I doubt thou art tottering on the
brink of ruin and desolation, this day! The nation is
all in a foment upon account of loosing dear Minorca.

Sunday, Aug. 15.—In the morn we got up about
five o'clock, and my wife, Sally, Tho. Davy, and
myself set out for the camp on Cox Heath, where we
arrived about ten o'clock, just as they were all got to
their devotions—to wit, twelve congregations, and
1000 in each congregation. They seemed to be very
attentive at their devotions, and minister seemed to
have a fine delivery. I think the camp as fine a sight as
I ever see.

[1] Minorca was taken by the French in the war waged by
Austria, France and Russia on one side against Frederick the
Great of Prussia and his brother-in-law George II (England). Admiral Byng was blamed for the loss of Minorca, was tried by
Court Martial and shot. Mr Turner's spelling, never his strong
point, goes completely to the bad under the influence of strong
emotion, or 'Bumboo'. F.M.T.

October 15.—My wife and I having fixed to go to Hartfield, my wife endeavoured to borrow a horse[1] of Jos. Fuller, Tho. Fuller, Will Piper, and Jos. Burgess, to no purpose, they having no reason for not doing it, but want of good nature and a little gratitude; tho' I make no doubt but they will, some or other of them, be so good natured as soon to come and say, 'Come, do write this land-tax or window-tax book for us'; then I always find good nature enough to do it, and at the same time to find them in beer, gin, pipes, and tobacco; and then, poor ignorant wretches, they sneak away, and omit to pay for their paper; but, GOD bless them, I'll think it proceeds more from ignorance than ill nature. My wife having hired a horse of John Watford, about four o'clock we set out on our journey for Hartfield, and as we were riding along near to Hastingford, no more than a foot's pace, the horse stood still, and continued kicking-up until we was both off, in a very dirty hole (but, thanks be to God, we received no

[1] Almost the only mode of getting about in Sussex in those days was on horseback, the husband riding with his wife on a pillion behind him. There was generally a narrow strip of road made hard by the refuse slag of the extinct iron works along which they jogged in winter, the rest of the road being available only in summer. B. and L. The roads were soon to improve as a result of the Turnpike Act; meanwhile they were mud paths treated with slag as here described. The Sussex iron industry was in its final decline as a result of timber depletion. Iron was first mined in a small way about 500 B.C. The Romans increased its exploitation and there were further great developments in the mid-thirteenth and mid-sixteenth centuries.

hurt). My wife was obliged to go in to Hastingford House, to clean herself. My wife and I spent the even at my father Slater's. We dined off some ratios of pork and green sallard.

*

Mrs. Slater[1] is a very Xantippe, having a very great volubility of tongue for invective, and especially if I am the subject; tho' what the good woman wants with me I know not, unless it be that I have offended her by being too careful of her daughter, who, poor creature, has enjoyed but little pleasure of her life in her marriage state, being almost continually, to our great misfortune, afflicted with illness.

*

This is the day, on which I was married and it is now three years since. Doubtless many have been the disputes which have happened between my wife and myself during the time, and many have been the afflictions which it has pleased GOD to lay upon us, and which we may have justly deserved by the many anemosityes and desentions which have been continually fermented between us and our friends, from allmost the very day of our marriage; but I may now say with the holy Psalmist, 'It is good for us that we have been afflicted'; for, thanks be to GOD, we now begin to live happy; and I am thoroughly persuaded,

[1] Mother-in-law.

9

if I know my own mind, that if I was single again, and at liberty to make another choice, I should do the same—I mean make her my wife who is so now.

Sunday, Dec. 26.—In the morning the Rev. Mr. Hamlin, of Waldron, preached at our church. We had an excellent sermon—Mr. Hamlin, in my opinion, being compleatest churchman of any clergyman in this neighbourhood, and who seems to take a great deal of pains in the discharge of his duty.

1757

On Sunday Jan. 9, 1757, died suddenly the Rev. Mr. Lyddell, rector of Ardingly, aged fifty-nine; a gentleman, who for his extensive knowledge, unlimited charity, general behaviour, and other amiable qualities, was an ornament to his profession, and yet so little publickly taken notice of, that he never enjoyed any church preferment except a small family living of one hundred pounds a year; he was possessed of a good paternal estate, above one thousand pounds a year, and tho' he lived in the most retired private manner, the yearly income of it was disposed of in assisting his friends in distress, and in charity to the poor. He dy'd a batchelor; the name is extinct. His estate devolves to Richard Clarke, Esq., of Blake Hall in Essex.

*

Oh, how dull is trade, how very scarce is money, never did I know so bad a time before. What shall I do! work I can not, and honest I will be, if the Almighty will give me grace.

May 7.—Perusing an abridgement of the *Life of Madame de Maintenon*, I find the following advise given her by her mother, Madame d'Aubigné, viz., to act in such a manner as fearing all things from men, and hoping all things from GOD.

22nd.—This afternoon there was a funeral sermon for Master Marchant, text—'Let me die the death of the righteous, and let my last end be like his.' From which words we had a very good sermon, tho' whether it was a funeral sermon they that preached it, and they that pay for it, alone must know; most of us thought it to be a sermon made before the death of Master Marchant.

June 14.—Master Durrant and I set out on foot for Lewes, to-day being the visitation. After church time, I was sworn with many more into my office of churchwarden, for which I paid 4*s*. 6*d*. After dinner we smoked our pipe.[1] I came home about ten P.M., thank GOD very safe and sober.

June 20.—This is my birthday, in which I enter the twenty-ninth year of my age; and may I, as I grow in years, so continue to increase in goodness; for, as my exit must every day draw nearer, so may I every day become more enamoured with the prospect of the happiness of another world, and more entirely dead

---

[1] The long clay 'churchwarden' pipe appears again on 2 January 1760, 10 May 1761 and 1 June 1764. Here it serves a ceremonial role after the swearing-in.

to the follies and vanities of this transitory world.

June 21.—Attended the funeral of Master Gold-smith at Waldron; this was the merriest funeral that ever I saw, for I can safely say there was no crying.

Sunday, July 10.[1]—The Right Honble. Geo. Cholmondely, Earl Cholmondely, Viscount Malpas, joint vice-treasurer of Ireland, lord lieutenant, cust. rot., and vice-admiral of Cheshire, governor of Chester Castle, lord lieutenant of Anglesea, Caernarvon, Flint, Merioneth, and Montgomery, steward of the royal manner of Sheen in Surrey, and Knight of the Bath, being a visiting at Mr. Coates's, was at church this morning.

Saturday, 30th.—I cannot say I think it prudent of my wife to go to Lewes now, as I look for the Duke of Newcastle down at Halland. I have several journeys to go next week, which I must postpone, on account of her absence. But, alas! what can be said of a woman's temper and thought? Business and family advantage must submit to their pride and pleasure; but tho' I mention this of women, it may perhaps be as justly applyed to men; but most people are blind to their own follies.

Sunday, Aug. 7.—This being a publick day at Halland I spent about two or three hours there in the afternoon, in company with several of our neighbours. There was a great company of people, of all

[1] Turner's interest in the nobility is evidenced here and in later entries; *The Peerage of England* was among his favourite reading.

denominations, from a duke to a beggar; among the rest of the nobility were his Grace the Duke of Newcastle, the Hon. Lord Cholmondely, Lord Gage, Earle of Ashburnham, the Lord Chief Justice Mansfield and Mr. Justice Dennison, and a great number of gentlemen. I was there three times this day. What a small pleasure it is to be in such a concourse of people! one hour spent in solitude being, in my opinion, worth more than a whole day in such a tumult; there being nothing but vanity and tumult in such public assemblies, and their being rather obstreperious than serious and agreeable. Oh! how silly is mankind, to delight so much in vanity and transitory joys!

Fryday, Aug. 12.—This day being the first race-day at Lewes, my sister Ann Slater[1] and I, upon a horse borrowed of Mr. French, rode to Lewes, where we arrived just as the people came from the hill. We went to see the ball, which, in my opinion, was an extreme pretty sight. The King's plate of 100 sovereigns was run for by Mr. Warren's horse Careless, and Mr. Roger's horse Newcastle Jack, which was won by Careless, the other being drawn after the first heat. 'Tis said there were £100 laid by the grooms that Careless beat the other six score yards, which he did.

Aug. 22.—I set off for Piltdown, where I saw Charles Diggens and James Fowle run twenty rod for one guinea each. I got never a bet, but very drunk.

Tuesday, 23rd.—Came home in the forenoon, not

[1] Sister-in-law.

13

quite sober; at home all day, and I know I behaved more like an ass than any human being—doubtless not like one that calls himself a Christian. Oh! how unworthy I am of that name.

Sunday, 28th.—My whole family at church. I think we have had too as good sermons to-day as I ever heard; Mr. Porter preached. Tho. Davy at our house in the even, to whom I read five of Tillotson's *Sermons.* [1]

Sept. 18.—My whole family at church—myself, wife, maid, and the two boys. We dined off a piece of boiled beef and carrots, and currant suet pudding; and we had, I think, too extreme good sermons this day preached unto us.

Sept. 20, 1756 [2]—In the even, Mr. Porter's hopers bought their pole-puller's nickcloth. [3]

Sept. 23.—Halland hop-pickers bought their pole-puller's nickcloth; and, poor wretches, many of them insensible.

Oct. 6.—This day how are my most sanguine hopes of happiness frustrated! I mean the happiness

[1] Archbishop John Tillotson (1630–94) was adjudged not only 'the best preacher of his age but also to have brought the art of preaching to perfection'. He became Archbishop of Canterbury in 1691. His style was plain and direct. See also 23 October and 27 November 1757, 4 January 1761 and 28 February 1762.

[2] If this is an error for 1757, the hop-pickers' revels must be to blame. But it may be that the entry (and its neighbours) are out of order in Blencowe and Lower's selection.

[3] Of rich and showy colour so that the other hop-pickers could see him easily.

between myself and wife, which hath now continued for some time; but, oh! this day it has become the contra! I think I have tryed all experiments to make our life's happy, but they have all failed. The opposition seems to be naturally in our tempers—not arising from spitefulness, but an opposition that seems indicated by our very make and constitution.

Tuesday, Oct. 11.—My brother and I set out for Battle market. I think Battle to be a pleasant situated town, and there seems to be a considerable market for stock; and the Abbey—which belongs to the family of the Websters and which was built just after the Conquest, in memory of the battle fought near that place between the Conqueror and Harold, in which the latter, his two brothers, most of the English nobility, and 97,974 common men (!) were killed—is the remains of a fine Gothic structure.

Monday, Oct. 17.—Tho. Durrant and I set out on our journey to Steyning, and arrived there in the even. Next day I settled with Mr. Burfield; after this we must needs walk up to Steyning town, where he had us about from one of his friend's houses to another, untill we became not very sober; but, however, we got back to Mr. Burfield's, and dined there. After dinner, thinking myself capable to undertake such a journey, I came away, leaving Tho. Durrant there, who actual was past riding, or amost any thing else. I arrived home, through the providence of GOD, very well, and safe, about seven; and, to give Mr. Burfield his just character, in the light wherein he appears to me, he is a very good-tempered man, a kind and affectionate husband, an indulgent and tender parent, benevolent and humane to a great degree, and who seems to have a great capacity and judgment in his business; but, after all, a man very much given to drink. When I came home, Dame Durrant was like to tare me to pieces, with words, for leaving her son behind; but it all came to rights with the assistance of two or three drams of her beloved Nantzy.[1] Steyning, I think, is but a small town, tho' both a borough and market town, and also a free grammar school there.

Oct. 26 (*Sunday*).[2] —This day, the holy sacrament being administered, my wife, self, and maid, all staid—my wife and I taking up a resolution, in the presence of Almighty God and Saviour, with his divine grace and holy Spirit, to forsake our sins, and to become better Christians, and to bear with each other's infirmityes, and live in peace with all mankind. Tho. Davy came in the evening, to whom I read six of Tillotson's *Sermons*.[3]

Oct. 24.—I went down to Jones's to the publick vestry.[4] It was the unanimous consent of all present to give to Tho. Daw, upon condition that he should buy the house in the parish of Waldron for which he

[1] French brandy from Nantes ('Nantz').
[2] An error for 23 October.
[3] See p. 14, note 1.
[4] A Monday evening meeting: vestry meetings were usually on Mondays.

hath been treating, by reason that he would then be an inhabitant of Waldron, and clear of our parish, halfe a tun of iron, £10; a chaldron of coals, &c., £2; in cash, £8; and find him the sum of £20, for which he is to pay interest, for to buy the said house: a fine present for a man that has already about £80; but yet, I believe, it is a very prudent step in the parish, for he being a man with but one leg, and very contrary withall, and his wife being entirely deprived of that great blessing, eyesight, there is great room to suspect there would, one time or other, happen a great charge to the parish, there being a very increasing family; and I doubt the man is none of the most prudent, he having followed smuggling very much in the past, which has brought him into a trifling way of life.

Oct. 31.—In the morn, Fielder brought our herrings, but could get no pandles;[1] I paid him for 1100 herrings, 33*s*.

Nov. 2.—Oh! how transient is all mundane bliss! I who, on Sunday last,[2] was all calm and serenity in my breast, am now nought but storm and tempest. Well might the wise man say, 'It were better to dwell in a corner of the house-top, than with a contentious woman in a wide house.'

Sunday, Nov. 27.—This day I compleated reading

[1] The old Sussex word 'pandle', now obsolete, means a shrimp; it is said to be derived from a Latin word *pandalus*. B. and L.

[2] This presumably refers to 30 October, but it could refer to 23 October.

of Tillotson's *Sermons*[1] over the second time. So far as I am a judge, I think them to be a compleat body of divinity—they being written in a plain familiar stile, but far from what may be deemed low.

Dec. 4.—This day compleated the reading of Sherlock *On Death*,[2] which I esteem a very plain good book, proper for every Christian to read—that is, rich and poor, men and women, young and old.

Dec. 5.—Mr. Gibbs paid me in full, £1. 3s. 9d. When he paid me, Mr. French and Tho. Fuller was in company of him; so that common civility obliged me to ask them to walk in, which they did, and staid till near nine o'clock; but I think nothing can be more frothey than these men's discourses.[3] Let us only think that they are all masters of families, and fathers

[1] See p. 14, note 1.

[2] A favourite among Sherlock's sermons, which also appear on 27 July 1760. Dr Thomas Sherlock (1678–1761) was successively Bishop of Bangor (1728), Salisbury (1734) and London (1748).

[3] An opinion shared by Dr John Burton (1751). He wrote: 'The farmers of the better sort are considered here as squires. These men however boast of an honourable lineage and look down on the rural vulgar. You would be surprised at the uncouth dignity of these men and their palpably ludicrous pride; the awkward prodigality and sordid luxury of their feasts; the inelegant roughness and dull hilarity of their conversation; their intercourse with servants so assiduous, with clergymen and gentlemen so rare; being illiterate they shun the learned, being sots the sober.' 'Iter Sussexiense', *Sussex Archaeological Collections*, vol. 8 (1856), p. 260. After his Sussex journey Dr Burton propounded in jest the theory that the long legs of Sussex folk and their animals might result from pulling them so often from the heavy mud! Cf. p. 8, note 1.

of many children, and yet their whole discourse seems turned to obscenity, oaths, gaming, and hunting; nothing to the improvement of the mind, nor the honour of God or man.

Dec. 12.—This day, died Mary Shoesmith, a childmaid at the Rev. Mr. Porter's, after about ten days' illness. This poor girl was cut off in the prime of her youth, not being seventeen. Oh! let mankind consider that no age nor sex is exempt from death! What is it that makes men so humble at the approach of death? Only their vices. Would they but refrain from evil and do good, and return unto the Lord their GOD, who hath promised mercy and forgiveness unto them that truly and sincerely repent, then the prospect of death would be but as a translation from a life of misery to an eternal state of happiness.

Sunday, Dec. 25.—Myself, the two boys, and servant at church; I and the maid staid the Communion. This being Christmas-day, the widow Marchant, Hannah, and James Marchant, dined with us, on a buttock of beef and a plumb suet pudding. Tho. Davy at our house in the even, to whom I read two nights of the *Complaint*, one of which was the 'Christian's Triumph against the Fear of Death:' a noble subject, it being the redemption of mankind by Jesus Christ. I think the author has treated it in a very moving and pathetic manner.

1758

1757.[1] *Jan*. 9.—Mr. Elless, Marchant, myself, and

[1] An error for 1758, natural at the beginning of a new year.

wife, sat down to whist about seven o'clock, and played all night: very pleasant, and, I think I may say, innocent mirth, there being no oaths nor imprecations sounding from side to side, as is too often the case at cards.

Jan. 11.—This day I gave a man 6*d.*, who came about a-beggin for the prisoners in Horsham Gaol, three of which are clergymen, two of them in for acting contrary to the laws of men, but not, in my opinion, to the laws of GOD—that is, for marrying contrary to the Marriage Act. The other is for stealing some linen; but, I hope he is innocent.

Jan. 20.—In the even I read a pamphlet, entitled *Primitive Christianity Propounded*, which I imagine was written by a Baptist preacher, in favour of preaching without notes.

I must say I can find no harm consequent on our method of reading, as the author is pleased to call it; but I must acknowledge that the idle, lazy, way of preaching which many of our clergy are got into, seems rather to prove self-interest to be the motive of the exercising their profession, than the eternal happiness and salvation of mankind.

Jan. 26.—We went down to Whyly, and staid and supped there; we came home between twelve and one o'clock—I may say, quite sober, considering the house we was at, though undoubtedly the worst for drinking, having, I believe, contracted a slight impediment in my speech, occasioned by the fumes of the liquor operating too furiously on my brain.

Jan. 28.—I went down to Mrs. Porter's, and acquainted her I could not get her gown before Monday, who received me with all the affability, courtesy, and good humour immaginable. Oh! what a pleasure would it be to serve them was they always in such a temper; it would even induce me, almost, to forget to take a just profit. In the even I read part of the *New Whole Duty of Man*.[1]

Feb. 2.—We supped at Mr. Fuller's and spent the evening with a great deal of mirth, till between one and two. Tho. Fuller brought my wife home upon his back. I cannot say I came home sober, though I was far from being bad company. I think we spent the evening with a great deal of pleasure.

Feb. 17.—This being the day appointed for a general fast and humiliation, myself, the boys, and servant, was at church in the morning. This fast-day hath, to all outward appearance, been observed in this parish with a great deal of decorum—the church in the morning being more thronged than I have seen it lately. Oh! may religion once more rear up her head in this wicked and impious nation!

Wednesday, 22nd.—About four P.M., I walked down to Whyly. We played at bragg the first part of the even. After ten we went to supper on four boiled chicken, four boiled ducks, minced veal, sausages,

---

[1] This Puritan book (anon. 1658) extolled the joys of Heaven far above those of earth; it was refuted by Tom Paine in *The Rights of Man* (1791) though his main target there was Burke's *Reflections on the French Revolution*.

21

cold roast goose, chicken pasty, and ham. Our company, Mr. and Mrs. Porter, Mr. and Mrs. Coates, Mrs. Atkins, Mrs. Hicks, Mr. Piper and wife, Joseph Fuller and wife, Tho. Fuller and wife, Dame Durrant myself and wife, and Mr. French's family. After supper our behaviour was far from that of serious, harmless mirth; it was down right obstreperious, mixed with a great deal of folly and stupidity. Our diversion was dancing or jumping about, without a violin or any musick, singing of foolish healths, and drinking all the time as fast as it could be well poured down; and the parson of the parish was one among the mixed multitude. If conscience dicatates right from wrong, as doubtless it sometimes does, mine is one that I may say is soon offended; for, I must say, I am always very uneasy at such behaviour, thinking it not like the behaviour of the primitive Christians, which I imagine was most in conformity to our Saviour's gosple. Nor would I be thought to be either a cynick or a stoick, but let social improving discourse pass round the company. About three o'clock, finding myself to have as much liquor as would do me good, I slipt away unobserved, leaving my wife to make my excuse. Though I was very far from sober, I came home, thank GOD, very safe and well, without even tumbling; and Mr. French's servant brought my wife home, at ten minutes past five.

Thursday, Feb. 25.[1]—This morning about six

[1] An error for 23 February. Alcohol is certainly responsible, as it is for the error in the date of the next entry (really 5 March).

o'clock just as my wife was got to bed, we was awaked by Mrs. Porter, who pretended she wanted some cream of tartar; but as soon as my wife got out of bed, she vowed she should come down. She found Mr. Porter, Mr. Fuller and his wife, with a lighted candle, and part of a bottle of wine and a glass. The next thing was to have me down stairs, which being apprized of, I fastened my door. Up stairs they came, and threatened to break it open; so I ordered the boys to open it, when they poured into my room; and, as modesty forbid me to get out of bed, so I refrained; but their immodesty permitted them to draw me out of bed, as the common phrase is, topsy-turvey; but, however, at the intercession of Mr. Porter, they permitted me to put on my ———, and, instead of my upper cloaths, they gave me time to put on my wife's petticoats; and in this manner they made me dance, without shoes and stockings, untill they had emptied the bottle of wine, and also a bottle of my beer. . . . About three o'clock in the afternoon, they found their way to their respective homes, beginning to be a little serious, and, in my opinion, ashamed of their stupid enterprise and drunken preambulation. Now, let any one call in reason to his assistance, and seriously reflect on what I have before recited, and they will join with me in thinking that the precepts delivered from the pulpit on Sunday, tho' delivered with the greatest ardour, must lose a great deal of their efficacy by such examples.

Sunday, March 3.—We had as good a sermon as

I ever heard Mr. Porter preach, it being against swearing.

Tuesday, March 7.—. . .[1] We continued, drinking like horses, as the vulgar phrase is, and singing till many of us were very drunk, and then we went to dancing and pulling wigs, caps, and hats; and thus we continued in this frantic manner, behaving more like mad people than they that profess the name of Christians. Whether this is consistent to the wise saying of Solomon, let any one judge: 'Wine is a mocker, strong drink is raging, and he that is deceived thereby is not wise.'

March 10.—Supped at Mr. Porter's, where the same scene took place, with the exception that there was no swearing and no ill words, by reason of which Mr. Porter calls it innocent mirth, but I in opinion differ much therefrom.

Saturday, March 11.—At home all day. Very piteous.

Friday, March 17.—. . . Now, I hope all revelling for this season is over; and may I never more be discomposed with so much drink, or by the noise of an obstreperious multitude, but that I may calm my troubled mind, and sooth my disturbed conscience.

March 23.—A very melancholy time occationed by the dearness of corn, tho' not proceeding from a

[1] The omitted beginning of this entry records that the same party as had forgathered on 22 February, with the addition of Mr Calverley and Mrs Atkins, met at supper at Mr Joseph Fuller's. B. and L.

real scarcity, but from the iniquitous practice of ingrossors, forestalling, &c. My trade is but very small, and what I shall do for an honest livelihood I cannot think; I am, and hope ever shall be, content to put up with two meals a day, and both of them I am also willing should be of pudding. As I am mortal, so have I my faults and failings in common with other mortals. I believe, by a too eager thirst after knowledge, I have oftentimes, to gratify that insatiable humour, been at to great expense in buying books, and spending rather too much time in reading;[1] for it seems to be the only diversion that I have any appetite for. Reading and study (might I be allowed the phrase) would in a manner be both drink and meat to me, was my circumstances but independent.

Sunday, April 2.—In the even, Master Hooke and myself went and searched John Jones's and Prawles', in order to see if there was any disorderly fellows, that we might have them to the setting to-morrow, in order to send them to sea.[2] We found none that we thought proper to send.

---

[1] Apart from religious and political works Turner's diverse reading included: Bishop Burnet's *History of the Reformation*; *The Life of Madame de Maintenon*; Homer's *Odyssey* (in translation); Boyle's lectures; *Paradise Lost*; Young's *Night Thoughts*; *Clarissa Harlow*; *Peregrine Pickle*; and Shakespeare's plays.

[2] The overstretched Navy suffered from chronic manpower shortage and this was a recognised form of impressment.

May 22.—As soon as I had breakfasted, I set out for Lewes, to commit the management of the debt due from Master Darby to me into the hands of Mr. Rideout. Oh, what a confusion and tumult there is in my breast about this affair! To think what a terrible thing it is to arrest a person, for by this means he may be entirely torn to pieces; but, on the other hand, this debt hath been standing above four years; they have almost quite forsaken my shop; I have just reason to suspect they must be deep in debt at other places, for no people of £200 a year go gayer than Mrs. Darby and her two daughters, and I at this time am so oppressed for want of money that I know not which way to turn.

Sunday, June 4.—About four o'clock, my wife and I set out for Lewes, on our roan mare, where we arrived about twenty minutes past seven. We went to see the Castle Mount, which I think a most beautiful sight, it being so well adorned with a great variety of shrubs and flowers, and so exceeding high that you have a command of the prospect of all the circumjacent country round. We came home, thank GOD, very safe, sober, and well, about thirty minutes past eight.

June 8.—A very melancholy time with me: my wife very ill, and I am prodigious uneasy about Master Darby's affair, for fear I should have been guilty of any harsh or inhuman usage. Oh! that I lived in solitude, and had not occation to act in trade, but still I hope and think I have done nought but what is consistent with self-preservation and the laws of equity.

June 10.—I went to Lewes on foot to know the result of Counsellor Humphrey's oppinion of Mr. Virgoe's will; and now what I am going to relate makes me shudder with horrour at the thoughts of it. It is, I got very much in liquor; but let me not give it so easy a name, but say I was very drunk, and in consequence no better than a beast. I got on horseback at the Cats, and proceeded on my way home, and met Mr. Langham and several more, but who they were I cannot remember. There was formerly a dispute between Mr. Langham and I, about a bill, and I imagine I must tell him of that. Whether they, seeing me more in liquor than themselves, put upon me, I do not remember; but Mr. Langham pulled me by the nose and struck at me with his horsewhip, and used me very ill. Mr. Adams told them he thought there was enough for a joke, upon which they used him very ill, and whilst they were a-fighting, I, free from any hurt, and like a true friend and bold hearty fellow, rode away upon poor Peter's horse, leaving him to shift for himself, and glad enough I got away with a whole skin. What can I say in my own behalf, for getting drunk? Sure I am a direct fool.

Monday, June 12.—A melancholy time, my wife at home very ill, trade very dull; but this is the hand of GOD, therefore I hope to bear it patiently.

Wednesday, June 14.—In the afternoon, at work in my garden; in the even, read the twelfth and last book of Milton's *Paradise Lost*, and which I have now read twice through, and in my opinion it exceeds anything I ever read, for sublimity of language and beauty of similies; and I think the depravity of human nature entailed upon us by our first parents is finely drawn.

Tuesday, June 20.—This is my birthday, on which I enter my thirtyeth year. How many, ere they have arrived at this age, have been cut off, probably in the midst of their sins! How careful should I be that I live not in vain—that, as I daily increase in age, so may I also improve in all virtue and godlyness of life! If we only look back and reflect upon the time that is past, we shall find him that lives to the greatest age will have room to say with holy Psalmist, that our days are past as it were a tale that is told; therefore my sincere wish is, that I may endeavour to lay hold on the present minute, that when my exit may be, I may ever more live a life of happyness and bliss.

June 22.—This day I saw in the *Lewes Journal*, that our troops under the command of the Duke of Marlborough had landed at St. Maloes,[1] and had burnt and otherwise destroyed 137 vessels of all denominations; and after destroying these vessels, he reimbarked his men without any loss. This success of our arms must doubtless greatly weaken and distress the French, who I believe are already in a very poor

[1] St Malo was no great event in itself, being chiefly a destruction of a nest of privateers; but it distracted France before the battle of Crefeld (see next entry).

way; but I do not imagine this to be a loss to the French nation adequate to the charge which our nation has been at in setting out and equipping such a fleet as ours; and yet I think it is acting a more humane part than burning and destroying a town, and thereby probably destroying, ruining, and taking away the life of many thousands of poor innocent wretches, that perhaps never did, nor thought of doing, any hurt to the British nation.

Thursday, June 29, 1758.—This day we had a rejoicing by ringing the bells, &c., for a victory gained over the French by Prince Ferdinand of Brunswick, near the Lower Rhine. Mr. Coates gave me an invitation to come down to-morrow night, to see him, and to rejoice on this occation. I think this is not the proper way of rejoicing, for I doubt there is little thoughts of returning thanks to Him that gives success in warr.

Friday, June 30.—I think I have a very great dread upon my spirits about to-night's entertainment; for, as I so seldom drink anything strong, I am thoroughly sensible a very little will make me drunk. Oh! a melancholy thing it is to deprive oneself of reason, and even to render ourselves beasts! But what can I do? If I goe, I must drink just as they please, or otherwise I shall be called a poor singular fellow. If I stay at home, I shall be stigmatized with the name of being a poor, proud, ill-natured wretch, and perhaps disoblige Mr. Coates . . .

We drank health and success to his Majesty and

the Royal Family, the King of Prussia, Prince Ferdinand of Brunswick, Lord Anson, his Grace the Duke of Newcastle and his Duchess, Lord Abergavenny, Admiral Boscawen, Mr. Pelham of Stanmore, the Earle of Ancram, Lord Gage, Marshall Keith, and several more loyall healths. About ten I deserted, and came safe home; but to my shame do I mention it very much in liquor. Before I came away, I think I may say there was not one sober person in company.

Now, let us seriously reflect upon this transaction, and look upon things in their proper light; and I doubt we shall find it a very improper way of rejoicing, instead of rejoicing in spirit and giving thanks and praises to Him who hath given our armies success in battle.

Sunday, July 2.—There was a brief read for to repair the groins and fortifications of the town of Brighthelmstone,[1] against the incroachments of the sea on that coast, which, if not timely prevented, will in all probability eat in and destroy the town, several houses having in a few years been swallowed up by the sea. Sadly disordered all day, not having recovered Friday night's debauch.

July 15.—A most prodigious mellancholy time, and very little to do. I think that luxury increases so fast in this part of the nation, that people have little or no money to spare to buy what is really necessary.

[1] The first move to develop the former fishing village into the famous health resort, Brighton.

The too-frequent use of spirituous liquors, and the exorbitant practice of tea-drinking has corrupted the morals of people of almost every rank.[1]

July 25.—Oh what a misfortune it is upon me my wife's being lame again, but let me not repine, since it is the Divine will. This is the twenty-ninth day on which we have had rain successively.

Wednesday, Aug. 2.—I compleated reading of Gay's *Fables*, which I think contains a very good lesson of morality; and I think the language very healthy, being very natural.

Thursday, Aug. 3.—In the even, the Duke of Newcastle came to Halland, as did Lord Gage, Sir Francis Poole, Mr. Shelley, Colonel Pelham, Mr. Pelham and several more, and stayed all night. What seems very surprising to me in the Duke of Newcastle, is, that he countenances so many Frenchmen, there being ten of his servants, cooks, &c., which was down here, of that nation.[2]

Saturday, Aug. 5.—Mr. Blake's rider called on me, and he and I rode together to Lewes, when I think I see the finest horse-race that ever I see run on that down or any other. There was four horses started for the purse of £50. There was a numerous, but I think not a brilliant, company. I came home in

[1] Yet tea was very dear in those days—14s. a pound and even more for best green tea, and 12s. and 10s. for Bohea. B. and L. See also p. 57, note 1.

[2] There was at Halland a room known as 'the Frenchmen's room'. B. and L.

company with Mr. Francis Elliss, about ten; but, to my shame do I say it, very much in liquor.

Sunday, Aug. 6.—Pretty bad all day, with the stings of a guilty and tormenting conscience.

Aug. 14.—At home all day, and, thank GOD, extremely busy. Was every day to be productive of as much busyness as to-day, I should in no wise envy the rich and great their continual rounds of ease and pleasure. No, it would add fresh vigour to my drooping spirits, and give an agreeable elasticity to my ardent desire of carrying on my trade with vigour; then would I exert my utmost power in buying in my goods, that I might run them out with a quick return.

Aug. 19.—I entertained my sister Sally, and my brother's wife, with the sight of the modern microcosm,[1] which I think is a very pretty curious sight, for we see the whole solar system move by clockwork, in the same manner they do in the heavens.

Aug. 23.—About four P.M., I walked down to Halland with several more of my neighbours, in order for a rejoicing for the taking of Cape Breton, &c., where there was a bonfire of six hundred of faggots, the cannon fired, and two barrels of beer given to the populace, and a very good supper

[1] The microcosm or 'orrery' was a clockwork-driven model planetarium devised by the great clockmaker-astronomer George Graham F.R.S. (1673–1751) and named in honour of Charles Boyle, 4th Earl of Orrery (1676–1731), soldier and writer. Graham was nephew and partner of Royal Clockmaker Thomas Tompion and was buried beside him in Westminster Abbey.

provided for the principal tradesman of this and the neighbouring parishes, as there had been a dinner for the gentlemen of Lewes and the neighbouring parishes. After supper we drank a great many loyall healths, and I came home in a manner quite sober. There was, I believe, near one hundred people entertained at Halland this day, besides the populace, and, so far as I see, everything was carried on with decency and regularity; tho' I must think the most proper way of rejoicing is by having a general thanksgiving, that the whole nation may give thanks to Him that gives success to our armies, both by sea and land; and I think, to shew our outward joy, it might be more properly done by distributing something to the poor.

Tuesday, Sept. 12.—At home all day. In the even I finished reading Salmon *On Marriage*, which I think to be a very indifferent thing, for the author appears to me to be a very bad logician.

Sept. 27.—In the morn, my brother and self set out for Eastbourne. We dined on a shoulder of lamb, roasted, with onion sauce—my family at home dining on a sheep's head, lights &c., boiled. We came home about ten P.M., but not sober. I may say, by the providence of GOD, my life was preserved, for, being very drunk, my horse took the wrong way, and ran into a travase[1] with me, and beat me off; but, thanks

---

[1] A 'travase' or 'traviss' in the Sussex vernacular was the shed adjacent to a blacksmith's shop in which horses were shod. B. and L.

be to GOD, I received no damage. . . . Oh, let me reflect how often, when I have been in liquor, I have been protected by the providence of Almighty GOD, and rescued from the jaws of death, and received no hurt; and how many instanties do we almost daily see of people's receiving hurt when in liquor; nay, even death itself has often, too, too often, been their unhappy lot!

Oct. 4.—In the forenoon I walked down in the park to look at an old pollard, from whence a swarm of bees had been taken. In the even, went down to Jones's, to make up the following trifling affair. Some time in the summer, Master Ball and a little boy of Riche's found a swarm of bees in Halland Park, which they agreed to divide between them, and they sent a person to Mr. Gibbs, to ask his consent to take the bees at the proper time for taking them. The fellow never saw Mr. Gibbs, but told them Mr. Gibbs gives his free consent. They, knowing no other than that they had the keeper's free consent, innocently enough proceeded to action. Some one told the keeper, and he before night committed it into the hands of an attorney. It was agreed that the men should pay 2s. 6d. each, the value of the honey and wax, spend 1s. each, and pay lawyer's letter, which they did; but sure it must appear hard in the keeper to use his power in so arbitrary a manner, for he owned that he was persuaded the men were honest; but he was determined to show his power, that no one for the future should dare transgress, or at least, if the law be open against them, they must expect to know something of the charge of law. But however, I think that, if shewing of power tend only to oppress the honest and industrious poor, as it did in the aforegoing cause, happy is the man that hath the least of it.

Oct. 7.—Oh, how happy must that man be whose more than happy lot it is to whom an agreeable company for life doth fall,—one in whom he sees and enjoys all that this world can give; to whom he can open the inmost recesses of his soul, and receive mutual and pleasing comfort to sooth those anxious and tumultuous thoughts that must arise in the breast of any man in trade! On the contrary, and I can speak from woful experience—how miserable must they be, where there is nothing else but matrimonial discord and domestic disquietude! How does these thoughts wrack my tumultuous breast, and chill the purple current in my viens! Oh, how are these delusive hopes and prospects of happiness before marriage turned into briers and thorns! But, as happiness is debarred me in this affair, I sincerely wish it to all those that shall ever tye the Gordian knot. Oh woman, ungrateful woman!—thou that wast the last and most compleatest of the creation, and designed by Almighty GOD for a comfort and companion to mankind, to smooth and make even the rough and uneven paths of life, art often, oh too, too often, the very bane and destroyer of our felicity! Thou not only takest away our happiness, but givest us, in lieu thereof, trouble and vexation of spirit.

Dec. 23.—At home all day. In the even I read part of Addison's *Evidences for the Christian Religion.* My wife a good deal indisposed with the pang in her side, and an ulcer on one of her legs. Oh, heavy and great misfortunes! But let me not repine, since it is the will of the Almighty.

Monday, Dec. 25.—This being Christmas-day, myself and wife at church in the morning. We stayed the Communion; my wife gave 6*d.*, but they not asking me I gave nothing. Oh, may we increase in faith and good works, and maintain and keep the good intentions that I hope we have this day taken up.

Fryday, Dec. 29.—Mr. French and I set out for Buxted Place. We were prodigious civilly entertained with some bread and cheese, wine and beer. We was showed the house all over, which undoubtedly is a very fine place, built in the modern taste. This even a meteor was seen in this neighbourhood, which appeared like a ball of fire falling from the clouds to the earth; it seemed as if it fell about Waldron, leaving a train of sparks behind it as it descended; its bigness was at least about the size of a large ball, tho' at first almost like a moon, and extremely light. I imagine fear and surprise hath exaggerated many of the above circumstances.

1759

Monday, Feb. 5, 1759.—In the even I went down

to the vestry; there was no business of moment to transact, but oaths and imprecations seemed to resound from all sides of the room; the sounds seemed to be harsh and grating, so that I came home soon after seven. I believe, if the penalty were paid assigned by the Legislature, by every person that swears that constitute our vestry, there would be no need to levy any tax to maintain our poor.

Feb. 7.—Molly Bell, Nanny Fuller, Frances Weller, Molly and Sam. French, and Lucy Durrant, together with Joseph Fuller and John French, supped at our house. We played at bragg, in the even, and I and my wife won 19*d*. They staid till thirty minutes past one, and went away all sober and in good order; and, what is very remarkable, there was not, that I could observe, one oath swore all the even. Huzza! The keeping of Christmas I hope is now over, and I think I was never more overjoyed; for, besides the expences attending it, there is something in it that is quite foreign to my taste or inclinations, I rather chusing a recluse and steady way of living, that may allow time for Reason to exercise her proper faculties, and to breath, as it were, into the mind of man a serener happiness, which, in my opinion, never can be enjoyed when it is so often disjointed and confused by such tumultuous or, at least, merry meetings.

Sunday, Feb. 11.—This I believe is as mild a time, considering the season of the year, as hath been known in the memory of man—everything having the appearance, and carrying with it the face of April, rather than of February (the bloom of trees only excepted); the meadows now are as verdant as sometimes they are in May, the birds chirping their melodious harmony, and the foot-walks dry and pleasant.

Fryday, Feb. 16.—This being the day appointed for a general fast, myself and servant went to church. The fast in this place hath seemingly been kept with great strictness, and I hope with sincere unaffected piety, our church in the morning being crowded with a numerous audience. I think no nation had ever greater occation to adore the Almighty Disposer of all events than Albion, whose forces meet with success in all quarters of the world. There now seems to reign a spirit of unity in our national councils; a king sitting upon the British throne, whose whole intentions seem to be that of making the happiness of every individual of his subjects, the same as his own. Let us all with sincerity and pure devotion, with one voice, continue to supplicate the blessing of the Almighty on this our happy Isle.

Sunday, April 22.—We had a sermon preached by the Rev. Mr. Thomas Hurdis, and again in the afternoon; and in my opinion he is as fine a churchman as almost I ever heard.

Sunday, May 13.—I went to church, and in the day and evening read two of Tillotson's *Sermons*,[1] and part of the second volume of Harvey's

[1] See p. 14, note 1.

Meditations. Oh, what a most delightful time it is, the birds tuning their melodious throats, and hymning their Creator's praise; whilst man, frail, degenerate man, lies supinely stretched on a bed of luxury and ease, or else is so immersed in the vain and empty pleasures of this world, that he is utterly forgetful of the goodness of the Supreme Being, that showers down His blessings upon him, and sheds plenteousness around his table.

Wednesday, May 30.—My wife very ill all day. Oh, melancholy time; what will become of me I cannot think! Very little trade, and she always so afflicted with illness; but let me not repine; possibly it is good for us that we have known affliction.

Saturday, July 7.—This day received by the post the disagreeable news of the French being landed at Dover; but yet I hope it is only a false report, set about by some credilous and fanciful people, without any real foundation. My wife very ill all day, and I think somewhat dangerous.

Monday, 9th.—I saw in the paper, that instead of our being invaded by the French, we have a fleet under the command of Admiral Rodney, now lying before Havre-de-Grace, bombarding the town, and had set it on fire in two places; so we have a sudden transition from sorrow to joy.

Sunday, July 29.—My family all at church in the afternoon. The text is the 24th verse of the 24th chapter of the Book of Joshua—'And the people said unto Joshua, The Lord our GOD will we serve, and his voice will we obey.' From which words we had an excellent sermon as I think I ever heard.

Wednesday, Aug. 1.—What quantityes of people begin to come down to Halland, and only to prepare and make ready a provision for luxury and intemperance against Sunday next, when, perhaps, hundreds of poor creatures are lamenting for want of sustenance and here shall be nothing but waste and riot.

Sunday, Aug. 5.—I spent most part of to-day in going to and from Halland, there being a public day, where there was to dine with his Grace the Duke of Newcastle, the Earls of Ashburnham and Northampton, Lord Viscount Gage, the Lord Abergavenny, and the two judges of assize, and a great number of gentlemen, there being, I think, upwards of forty coaches, chariots, &c. I came home about seven, not thoroughly sober. I think it is a scene that loudly calls for the detestation of all serious and considerating people, to see the sabbath prophaned, and turned into a day of luxury and debauchery; there being no less than ten cooks, four of which are French, and perhaps fifty more, as busy as if it had been a rejoicing day. There was such huzzaing[1] that made the very foundations (almost) of the house to shake, and all this by the order and approbation of almost the next man to the King. Oh, what countenance does such behaviour in a person of his Grace's rank,

[1] Celebration of the victory at Minden (1 August) probably enlivened this Public Day.

40

give to levity, drunkenness, and all sorts of immorality!

Aug. 15.—This day his Majestie's purse of £105 was run for, on Lewes Downs, when only Lord Portman's horse, Bosphorus, started for the same. There was also a bye-match run, for a considerable sum, between the Duke of Richmond's grey horse, Muli Ishmael, and Sir Mathew Featherstonhaugh's[1] grey mare, Sally, which was won by the former with great difficulty, he not beatting by above half a length, and at the same time the knowing ones was very much taken in.

Oct. 20.—In the even, read the *Extraordinary Gazette* for Wednesday, which gives an account of our army in America, under the command of General Woolf, beating the French army under General Montcalm, near the city of Quebec, wherein both the generals were killed, as also two more of the French generals; and the English General Monkton, who took the command after General Woolf was killed, was shot through the body, but is like to do well; as also the surrender of the city of Quebec. Oh, what a pleasure it is to every true Briton, to see with what success it pleases Almighty GOD to bless his Majestie's arms, they having success at this time in Europe, Asia, Africa, and America! I think in this affair, our generals, officers, and common men, have behaved with uncommon courage and resolution, having many and great difficulties to encounter

[1] Squire of Uppark, and neighbour of the Duke at Goodwood.

before they could bring the city to surrender.

Sunday, Oct. 28.—Both at Framfield and Hothly we had a thanksgiving prayer for the success with which it has pleased Almighty GOD to bless his Majestie's arms; and, in my opinion, it was extremely well composed.

Thursday, Nov. 15.—After dinner set out for Allfriston, in company with James Marchant, Durrant, and Tho. Davy—they on foot, myself on horseback; the intention of our journey was purely to see Mr. Elliss. We supped with him at his lodgings, and plaid at bragg in the even; and, though we plaid as low a game as possible, it was my unhappy lot to loose 3*s*. I think almost to give over ever playing at cards again. If we reflect how much more service this 3*s*. would have done, had it been given to some necessitous and industrious poor, than fooled away in this manner, I was not a-doing right when I was a-loosing it. We spent the evening and night, till past three o'clock, and, excepting my lost, extreme agreeable; for we had plenty of good liquor, and a hearty welcome, and no swearing or quarrelling, but all seemed prodigiously delighted with each other's company, and at the same time we went to bed sober.

Saturday, Dec. 8.—I walked down to Halland, there being rejoicing, on account that Admiral Hawk hath dispersed a fleet which was preparing to invade this nation. This engagement is looked on as a great advantage, as it has intirely dispersed the fleet, and wholly disconcerted their schemes, so that probably their thoughts of invading these nations must be laid by for some time. We drank a great many loyal toasts. I came home after eleven, after staying in Mr. Porter's wood[1] near an hour and an half, the liquor opperating so much in the head that it rendered my leggs useless. Oh, how sensible I am of the goodness of the Divine Providence, that I am preserved from harm!

Fryday, Dec. 21.—We arose at three, to perform our task, viz.: some of the ancestors of the Pelham family have ordered that, on this day (for ever) there should be given to every poor man or woman that shall come to demand it, 4*d*.; and every child, 2*d*.; and also to each a draught of beer, and a very good piece of bread. I believe there was between seven and eight hundred people relieved, of all ages and sexes, and near £9 distributed, besides a sack of wheat made into good bread, and near a hogshead and half of very good beer.

1760

Wednesday, Jan. 2, 1760.—Joseph Fuller and Mr. Thornton smoked a pipe[2] with me in the even. Oh,

---

[1] The Rector's wood was also known as 'the Breeches Wood', having been given to a previous Rector by a lady parishioner who was concerned by the constant state of disrepair of the rectorial breeches. Note that the diarist takes some 'shagg' (strong rough cloth) for a pair of breeches for Mr Porter (10 April 1755). In the Overseer's accounts for 1777 is a receipt for a payment to Rev. Thomas Porter for 'faggots for the poor'. (This should have helped to keep him 'well-breeched'!)

[2] See p. 11, note 1.

how pleasant has this Christmas been kept as yet; no revelling, nor tumultuous meetings, where there too often is little else but light and trifling discourse; and it's well if it is not intermixed with some obscene talk, and too often with vile and execrable oaths. Not that I am any ways an enemy to innocent mirth; but, what I protest against, is that which is not so.

Thursday, Jan. 24.—Went to Mr. French's, where I plaid at brag till supper; I and my wife lost 3*s.* 7*d.* Thank GOD, very sober, as was all the company (except Dame Durrant).

*

We plaid at bragg in the evening and staid (the usual party) till twenty minutes to two, and not a person in company sober; and I am sure, to my own shame, I was as bad as any one . . . the company seeming to be wonderfully pleased with their entertainment, exhillarated my spirits, so that I was transported beyond the natural bounds of my temper, and by that means I was left destitute of reflection and caution.

Saturday, March 8.—This day a melancholy affair broke out in this neighbourhood. Lucy Mott, servant to Mr. French, last night absconded herself from his service, privately, and quite unknown to any one in the family, and, from many corroborating circumstances, there is great probability that she hath committed the rash act of suicide. She went off in her worst apparel, and left behind her all her money, and had taken more than common care in laying up all her cloths, and collecting them together, so that it might be the more easy to find them by her relations. There is also the greatest reason imaginable to think that she was pregnant.

Monday, April 7.—After dinner I went down to Jones, to the vestry. We had several warm arguments at our vestry to-day, and several vollies of execrable oaths oftentime redouned, from allmost all parts of the room. A most rude and shocking thing at publick meetings.

Fryday, June 21.—This day hath been my birth-day,[1] and that on which I enter into the thirty-second year of my age; and may the GOD of all mercy and goodness pour into my heart the graces of his holy Spirit, that, as I grow in years, so I may increase in goodness, and daily be renewed in the inner man.

July 9.—In the afternoon my wife walked to Whitesmith, to see a mountybank perform wonders, who has a stage built there, and comes once a week to cuzen a parcel of poor deluded creatures out of their money, by selling his packets, which are to cure people of more distempers than they ever had in their lives, for 1*s*. each, by which means he takes sometimes £8 or £9 of a day.

Sunday, July 27.—In the even and the day read six of Bishop Sherlock's *Sermons*,[2] which I think extremely good, there being sound reasoning in them,

---

[1] Elsewhere 20 June. See p. 3, note 2.
[2] See p. 18, note 2.

and seem writ with an ardent spirit of piety, being mostly levelled against Deists.

Saturday, Aug. 13.—At home all day, and, thank GOD, pritty busy. Oh, what pleasure it is to have some trade; how does it enliven one's spirits!

Fryday, Oct. 3.—At home all day, and thank GOD, pretty busy, but my wife very ill. Oh, how mellancholy a time it is! quite destitute of father and mother, and am in all probability like to loose my wife, the only friend, I believe, I have now in this world, and the alone center of my worldly happiness. When I indulge the serious thought, what imagery can paint the gloomy scene that seems just ready to oppen itself, as it were, for a theatre for my futer troubles to be acted upon!

Tuesday, Oct. 7.—In the even there was a rejoicing at Halland, and a bonfire, for our army under the command of General Amherst having taken Montreal and all Canada from the French. All the neighbourhood were regaled with a supper, wine, punch, and strong beer. To-day I sent Thomas Durrant to Brighthelmstone for Dr. Poole, who came to my wife in the even. She is prodigiously ill. At home all day, and, thank GOD, pretty busy.

Sunday, Oct. 26.—To-day we had the melancholly newes of the death, by a fit of the apoplexy, of his most august Majesty George II., king and parent of this our most happy isle; had his Majesty lived to the 10th of November, he would have been seventy-seven years of age. He has sit upon the British throne thirty-three years the 22nd of last June.

Sunday, Dec. 21.—No service at our church in the morn, Mr. Porter preaching at Laughton; Dr. Poole, coming to see a child of his, paid my wife a visit, and charged me 10s. 6d.: really a fine thing it is to be a physician, who can charge as they please, and not be culpable according to any human law.

Sunday, 28th.—We had a sermon preached by a young clergyman just come to be curate at Laughton and I imagine this to be the first time of his preaching. We had, in my oppinion, a learned sermon; and I think if the young gentleman's morals are good, he will in time make a fine man. My wife, thank GOD, something better; in the even I read Gibson *On Lukewarmness in Religion*, and a sermon of his, intitled *Trust in God the best Remedy against Fears of all kinds*: both of which I look upon as extreme good things.

1761

Jan. 4, 1761.—No service at our church in the morning, on account of the death of Mrs. Porter.[1] In the even I read three of Tillotson's *Sermons*[2] to Tho. Davey.

Saturday, Jan. 17.—We dined on the remains of yesterday's dinner, with the addition of some sausages, broiled. Oh, my poor wife is most

[1] This casual entry reflects Turner's personal concern about his wife, Peggy. Mr Porter evidently remarried: see reference to a Mrs Porter alive on 8 December 1771 in the Appendix, p. 83.

[2] See p. 14, note 1.

prodigious bad! No, not one gleam of hope have I of her recovery. Oh, how does the thought distract my tumultuous soul! What shall I do?—what will become of me!

Sunday, Feb. 21.[1]—I called on Mr. Verral[2] and Mr. Scrase,[3] and came home at thirty minutes past six. Oh, could I say sober! Oh, how weak is nature—at least corrupt and fallen nature! But what I most stand aghast at is to think how miserable must my unhappy lot speedily be, should I sleep never to open my eyes again in this world when ever I am in liquor.

March 30.—This day died John Brown, after a few hours' illness, aged thirty. Oh, what a lesson on mortality! What poor negligent and heedless creatures too many of us are, that we cannot learn, from such striking instances, to live in such a manner that we may not be affraid to meet death whenever it may happen!

April 6.—Oh, how glad am I that the hurry and confusion is over at Halland, for it quite puts me out of that regular way of life which I am so fond of, and not only so, but occasions me, by too great hurry of spirits, many times to comit such actions as is not agreeable to reason and religion.

[1] An error for 22 February.

[2] One of this name engaged in controversy in Lewes with Tom Paine about the Prussian King Frederick. Paine was an exciseman there at the time; he was apparently unrelated to the surgeon, Nathaniel Paine.

[3] See also Appendix, p. 81

In the morn[1] down at Halland, where there was, I believe, near five hundred people to attend his Grace to Lewes—the election being there for the county, to-day, but no opposition.

April 19.—My wife somewhat easier to-day, tho' still very bad, and dangerous.

April 28.—There being at Jones's a person with an electrical machine,[2] my niece and I went to see it; and tho' I have seen it several years agoe, I think there is something in it agreeable and instructing, but at the same time very surprising. As to my own part, I am quite at a loss to form any idea of the phœinomina.

Whitsunday, May 10.—Myself at church in the morn; I staid the Communion; gave 6*d.* Myself and servant at church in the afternoon. Sam Jenner and Tho. Durrant drank tea with me, and after tea we walked over to Chiddingly, to see a house which was repairing there. Walked into Mr. Robert Turner's, where we staid and smoked two serious pipes,[3] and came home about nine. As pleasant an even as I ever walked in my life.

Sunday, May 17.—This day was buryed at our church, Francis Rich, aged forty-five years, who died after a few days ilness, and has left a wife and seven children. What a moving spectacal it was to see an in-dustryous and sober man, the only support of his

[1] Tuesday 7 April.

[2] This was the glass friction electricity generator of Francis Hauksbee (Hawksbee), brought out in 1709. Its production of sparks made it a source of entertainment.

[3] See p. 11, note 1.

family, followed to the grave by his widow and fatherless infants, whose tears and lamentations bespoke their inward and sincere grief!

June 10.—Was fought this day, at Jones's, a main of cocks, between the gentlemen of Hothly and Pevensey. *Quere*, Is their a gentleman in either of the places that was consernd?

June 17.—This day Mr. Porter administered the communion to my wife, and self, and servant; this, in all human probability, will be the last time we shall ever commemorate together, in this world, the death of our Blessed Saviour and Redeemer.

June 23.—About five o'clock in the afternoon, it pleased Almighty GOD to take from me my beloved wife, who, poor creature, has laboured under a severe tho' lingering illness for these thirty-eight weeks, which she bore with the greatest resignation to the Divine will. In her I have lost a sincere friend, a virtuous wife, a prudent good economist in her family, and a very valuable companion. I have lost an invaluable blessing, a wife who, had it pleased GOD to have given her health, would have been of more real excellence to me than the greatest fortune this world can give. I may justly say, with the incomparable Mr. Young, 'Let them whoever lost an angel, pity me.'

July 26.—After dinner we all walked down to Halland, were there was a public day. We staid and walked about till near eight o'clock. I lodged at Joshua Durrant's, and my brother and Mr. Tomlin lodged at my house, tho' not one of us went to bed sober; which folly of mine makes me very uneasy. Oh, that I cannot be a person of more resolution!

July 27.—Very bad all the even. Oh, my heavy and troubled mind! Oh, my imprudence pays me with trouble!

July 28.—I am intollerable bad: my conscience tears me in pieces.

Aug. 5.—Almost distracted with trouble: how do I hourly find the lost I have sustained in the death of my dear wife! What can equal the value of a virtuous wife? I hardly know which way to turn, or what way of life to pursue. I am left as a beacon on a rock, or an ensign on a hill.

Nov. 24.—At home all day, and very busy. Oh, what pleasure is business! How far preferable is an active busy life, when imployed in some honest calling, to a supine and idle way of life, and happy are they whose fortune it is to be placed where commerce meets with incouragement, and a person has the opportunity to push on trade with vigor.

Dec. 11.—This day was brought home by two men, whom the parish had sent on purpose, Will. Burrage, who had absconded about five years ago, and left a wife and six small children as a burthen to the parish. Now, as the affair makes a great noise, and the inhabitants seem much divided in their oppinion about the treatment which he deserves, I shall for the futer satisfaction of any one who may happen to see my memoirs, deliver my own sentiments on the affair.[1] First Mr. Porter, Mr. Coates, and Mr. French, are desirous he should suffer the punishment due to so atrocious a crime as deserting his family, by which means they have cost the parish upwards of £50, and the poor woman become a lunatic, through grief, in the most rigorous manner; the rest of the people are all desirous that he should escape without any further punishment, and they plead that it will be of no service to the parish to confine him in the House of Correction. This I think savours too much of a contracted and self-interested mind. Neither of these methods do I approve of. I would then advise that justice should take place in such a manner that strict eye may be had to mercy, and not in the height of executive justice to forget the bening virtue. . . . . In my oppinion justice with humanity should first be executed, and then let mercy and benevolence open their extended wings, and close the scene.

1762

Monday, Jan. 25, 1762.—Imployed myself to-day part of the day in sawing of wood. Oh, melancholly time! what to do I hardly know. I am come as it were to a resolution to leave this place.

Jan. 27.—The wife of Tho. Davy was this day delivered of a girl, after being married only six months; two people whom I should the least have suspected of

---

[1] This passage emphasises that, while Turner's diary was primarily personal, he entertained hopes that others might read it in the years to come. See also 15 April 1765.

being guilty of so indiscreet an act. But what can be said of this passion?—how careful should we be of ourselves in this particular, when we daily see people of the strictest virtue apparently guilty of it.

Feb. 20.—In the even I walked down to Tho. Davy's (by whom I had been earnestly solicited to come), his infant daughter being baptized in the afternoon; I staid and spent the even there in company with Tho. Durrant, Ann Dallaway, James Marchant, Elizabeth Mepham, and Mr. John Long. Came home about three minutes past twelve—sober. Oh, how comfortable does that word sober sound in my ears!

Feb. 22.—At home all day. A more melancholy time in trade I never knew in my life, and I believe it to be the same throughout the county; and, what still renders it the more unpleasant, no friend, no not one, with whom I can spend an hour to condole and sympathize with me in my affliction.

Sunday, Feb. 28.—Myself and both servants at church in the afternoon; at home all the day, read part of Drelincourt *On Death*,[1] and in the even, one of Tillotson's *Sermons*.[2]

Fryday, March 12.—This being the day appointed for a General Fast and Humiliation before Almighty God, myself and both the servants were at church in

[1] This heavy dull book had no sale till Defoe set it in motion by that best of all ghost stories 'A True Relation of the Apparition of one Mrs Veal, the next day after her death, to one Mrs Bargrave, of Canterbury'. It ran through forty editions after it had been strongly recommended by the ghost of Mrs Veal. B. and L.

[2] See p. 14, note 1.

the morn; we had a very crouded audience, and un-doubtedly a very good sermon.

March 25.—Joseph Fuller, Tho. Durrant, and Tho. Long, came and smoked a pipe with me in the even. Oh, how does the memory of that ever-valuable creature, my deceased wife, come over my thoughts as it were a cloud in May! Who is that man that has once been in the possession of all this world can give to make happy and then to lose it, but must ever and again think of his former happiness?

March 28, *Sunday.*—In the morn I set out for Hartfield and dined with my father Slater, and came home at five minutes past six; I cannot say thoroughly sober—I think it almost impossible to be otherwise with the quantity of liquor I drank . . . But, however much in liquor I was, my reason was not so far lost but I could see a sufficient difference at my arrival at my own house between the present time and that of my wife's life, highly to the advantage of the latter. Everything then was serene and in order; now, one or both servants out, and everything noise and confusion. Oh! it will not do. No, no! it will never do.

Sunday, April 4.—We had a Thanksgiving Prayer read to-day, for the success attending his Majesty's armies in the reduction of that important island of Martinico, which has lately surrendered unto his Majesty's generals employed in that expedition.

Sunday, May 16.—No service at our church in the afternoon; myself and one of the servants walked to

Little Horsted Church, where we had a sermon preached by the Rev. Mr. Philips, curate of that parish and Maresfield, from the 10th, 11th, 12th and 13th verses of the second chapter of the Song of Solomon. We had, I think, as good if not the best sermon I ever heard, both for eloquence of language and soundness of divinity—the gentleman discoursing on the words in a very spiritual manner, so that I really think it quite a masterly performance. A very fine, pleasant day. Oh, how pleasant is this season of the year; all nature wears the livery, as it were, of gayety.

Sunday, Aug. 1.—There being only prayers in our church, Sam Jenner and I took a ride to Seaford, where we took a walk by the seaside, and took a view of two forts newly erected there, one of which has five 24-pounders mounted, and the other five 12-pounders.[1] We came home about ten P.M.; Oh, could I say thoroughly sober! I was not so far intoxicated to-day as to be guilty of any indiscretion, but still, tho' we only took a ride with no other design than an innocent, inoffensive amusement, and with an intention of reaping the advantage of serious and improving conversation, yet, being guilty of this one folly, the whole of our journey must become contaminated.

[1] Seaford was a vulnerable area and in Napoleonic times these forts were superseded by a Martello tower, which is still there. As a result of the destruction of the French fleet at Quiberon under Hawke on 20 November 1759 these two forts were already superfluous before 1760.

Sunday, Aug. 8.—Myself and servant at church in the morning and afternoon. How much more pleasure is it to be at home all day of a Sunday and to attend the service of the church, than to be rioting about as I have been too much of late; but may I never more offend in that point.

Thursday, Aug. 12.—This morning about thirty minutes past seven, her Majesty Queen Charlotte, consort of our most gracious Sovereign, was safely delivered of a Prince, and are both like to do well.

Aug. 13—This day the King's plate of £100 was run for on Lewes Downs, by Lord Grosvenor's horse, Boreas, and Mr. Howard's cross mare, Sukey, which was won by Boreas distancing the mare the first heat.

Aug. 14.—This day the purse of £50 was run for, when Mr. Wildman's horse, Lincoln, Mr. Tod's gelding, Janus, Mr. Blackman's mare, Slouching Sally, and Mr. Wilson's mare, Harmless, started; which was won by Lincoln, he getting the two first heats.

Aug. 23.—Thank God I have been very busy all day, I may say the busiest day I have known this many a day. Oh, what pleasure it is to be busy; it quite charms the spirits and chases away the gloom that hangs on a melancholy brow! My old, I wish I could say my worthy, friend, Mr. Tucker of Lewes came to dine with me.

Oct. 31.—No service at our church in the morning or afternoon. I dined on a roasted goose and apple sauce; I drank tea with Mr. Carman and his family.

This is not the right use that Sunday should be applied to. No, it is not.[1]

1763

Jan. 29. 1763.—The frost began to thaw to-day, after having continued very severe for five weeks; the ice was seven inches thick.

March 24.—I went to Jones's, there being a vestry holden there to make a poor rate. We staid till near one o'clock, quarrelling and bickering, about nothing. The design of our meeting was to have made a poor rate, every one to be assessed to the racked rent. But, how do I blush to say, what artifice and deceit, cunning and knavery, was used by some to conceal their rents. I look upon that man, be him who he will, that endeavours to evade the payment of his just share of taxes, to be a robbing every other member of the community that contributes his quota.

Thursday, May 5.—This was the day appointed by authority for a general thanksgiving for the late peace. No service at our church in the morn, Mr. Porter being on a journey. We have had no kind of rejoicing in this place, tho' it is the day for the proclamation of peace. I think almost every one seems to be dissatisfied with this peace, thinking it an ignominious and inglorious one. Read Shakespeare's *As you Like It*, and *Taming of the Shrew*, both of which I think good comedies.

[1] Tea is mentioned six times in the diary, usually with a disfavour surely related to its luxury price.

June 23.—This day two years ago was the day on which it pleased Almighty GOD to take from me my dear wife, during which interval of time the world has many times discovered that I have been on the point of marriage; but I am clear in this, that I have never yet made any offers of love to any one woman; no not anything like courting; not that I have made any resolution to live single. If ever I do marry again, I am sure of this, that I shall never have a more virtuous and prudent wife than I have been already possessed of; may it be the will of Providence for me to have as good an one; I ask no better.

June 28.—In the even, Joseph Fuller and myself plaid a game of cricket with Mr. Geo. Banister and James Fuller, for half a crown's worth of punch which we won very easy, but it being hot and drinking a pretty deal of punch, it got into my head, so that I came home not sober.

June 29.—Very stiff and disagreable to myself upon my game of cricket last night. In the even read part of Beveridge's *Thoughts.*

July 13.—In the even read several political papers called the *North Briton,*[1] which are wrote by John

[1] John Wilkes M.P. entered Parliament in 1757 and in 1762 started a series of bitter attacks on Lord Bute in the *North Briton.* No 45 was adjudged 'seditious libel' by the House of Commons and Wilkes had to fly to France. He was excluded from the House for some years and supported the Colonists during the American War of Independence. He was the popular idol of his day; though a radical he became Lord Mayor of London after regaining his place in Parliament in 1774.

Wilks, Esq., member for Ailsbery in Bucks, for the writing of which he has been committed to the Tower, and procured his release by a writ of *Harbus Corpus*. I really think they breath forth such a spirit of liberty, that it is an extreme good paper.

Saturday, Sept. 17.—In the afternoon, about three minutes past five, died Mr. French, after a long and lingering illness, which its to be doubted was first brought on by the to frequent use of spirituous liquors, and particularly gin. If it was possible to make any estimate of the quantity he drank for several years, I should think he could not drink less, on a moderate computation, than twenty gallons a year. Let me from such instances fly the habit of drinking, and think upon final consequences. Mr. French was aged fifty-five years.

Sept. 26.—I never knew any place so much gone of for trade as this is, since I have lived in it most of the principal inhabitants, as we esteem them, being dead, and those remaining so reduced, that trade is got to be very triffling. Custom has brought tea and spirituous liquors so much in fashion, that I dare be bold to say, they often, to often, prove our ruin, and I doubt often, by the too frequent use of both, entail a weakness upon our progeny.

Nov. 10.—Let me once more describe my uneasy situation, but at the same time acknowledge the many blessings of Providence which I enjoy, far superior to many of my fellow creatures, perhaps far more deserving of them than myself; but, alas! what afflicts me is the loss of my dear Peggy. . . . For want of the company of the more softer sex, and through my over much confinement, I know I am become extreme awkard, and a certain roughness and boisterousness of the disposition has seized on my mind, so that, for want of those advantages which flow from society, and a free intercourse with the world, and a too great delight in reading, has brought my mind to that great degree of moroseness that is neither agreable to myself, nor can my company be so to others.

Nov. 24.—Mr. Banister having lately taken from the smugglers[1] a freight of brandy, entertained Mr. Carman, Mr. Fuller, and myself, in the even, with a bowl of punch.

Nov. 25.—Mr. ——, the curate of Laughton, came to the shop in the forenoon, and he having bought some things of me (and I could wish he had

[1] Smuggling in Sussex reached high peaks of activity during both the Seven Years' War and the Napoleonic Wars. The incitement and the opportunities were maximal in each period, the Prevention resources being much depleted by the demands of the services. Almost the whole population participated, including the clergy, who were often won over by a keg of 'Nantzy' (see p. 16, note 1). A story is told of a parish clerk near Brighton who told his Rector, 'You can't preach today, sir.' As it was the Sabbath he was asked why, and promptly replied: 'The church is full of kegs and the pulpit's full of tea!' After 1830 the Preventive Service was much strengthened, and after a series of bloody battles on the beaches smuggling slowly declined.

Brandy took a high place among contraband but tea, tobacco, silks, coffee, cocoa and chocolate were freely smuggled as well as home products like candles, leather, salt and soap.

paid for them), dined with me, and also staid in the afternoon till he got in liquor, and being so complaisant as to keep him company, I was quite drunk. How do I detest myself for being so foolish!

Dec. 7.—I think since I have lived at Hothly I never knew trade so dull or money so scarce, the whole neighbourhood being almost reduced to poverty.

Dec. 26.—Jno. Vine and Edwd. Hope were elected surveyors for the ensuing year; and I think, had we try'd all Sussex, or even England, for to have found two such, we could not have done it: people very improper to serve the office, being litigious in the extremest degree, and withall very ill-natured, executing law to the utmost; but in the midst of law they quite forget justice, equity, or charity.

1764

Jan. 11.—This morn was found dead, in our parish, William Ludlow, belonging to Chiddingly, supposed to drop on accont of his being in liquor, and to have perished by the inclemency of the weather. How should such instances as these teach mankind to shun that hateful vice of drunkenness—a crime almost productive of all other vices!

Sunday, Feb. 19, 1764.—I read to my friend Sam. Jenner, a part of three discourses, wrote by James Walker, a Baptist preacher, the last of which I esteem the best performance, it being, in my judgement, wrote with a true spirit of piety, and in a pretty modest stile; and what may, I presume, be proper to be read by any sect whatsoever, there being nothing more in it than what it is the duty of all Christians both to practice and believe. Perhaps it may appear odd, Sam. Jenner being so much at my house; but he being a good-natured, willing person, who oftimes does my gardening, &c., for nothing, he is undoubtedly a worthy companion. I must own that my friend Joseph[1] is rather too fruitful in his invention to contrive some way to get a little liquor, or a pipe or two of tobacco.

April 12.—In the afternoon I walked to Uckfield, to pay my friend Mr. Elliss a visit, with whom I drank tea, and spent the even, and came home very safe and well, and pretty sober, about ten; and I think I never was entertained in so polite and genteel a manner by any one person I ever paid a visit to—everything being conducted with the greatest politeness imaginable, and yet with the greatest freedom and friendship!

April 28.—After breakfast, Mr. Hill and I set out for Maidstone. We went to see Mereworth Place, and Church: the first, the seat of the late Earls of Westmoreland, but now Lord Despencer's, and I think the seat as beautiful a little seat as I ever see, there being a great deal of extreme good painting, some very fine marble, and everything of ornament very noble. The church is modern built, and excessively handsome,

---

[1] Alcohol is almost certainly responsible for this misnomer: we are still concerned with Samuel Jenner.

but small.

May 2.—This day was fought a main of cocks, at our public-house, between the gentlemen of East Grinstead and the gentlemen of East Hothly, for half-a-guinea a battle and two guineas the odd battle, which was won by the gentlemen of East Grinstead, they winning five battles out of six fought in the main. I believe there was a great deal of money sported on both sides.

Sunday, May 13.—Myself, Mr. Dodson, and servant at church in the morn. During the time we was at church, Mr. Richardson and my brother came to see me. We dined on a calf's heart pudding, a piece of beef, greens, and green sallet.[1] Mr. Joseph Hartley came to bring me a new wigg. Paid him in full for a new wigg, £1. 15*s*., and new mounting an old one, 4*s*.

Sunday, May 20.—We had a vestry called, and we stayed in the church-yard to consult whether we should lend Francis Turner the sum of six guineas on the parish account, in order for him to discharge a debt for which he is threatened with an arrest, if the same is not paid to-morrow; when it was the unanimous consent of all present to lend him the said sum. After churchtime, Mr. Dodson and I walked down to ask Sam Jenner how he did, with whom we staid and drank tea; a very fine pleasant day; but when I consider the nature of my circumstances, that there is no one person to whom I may entrust the

[1] The contemporary spelling of 'salad'.

management of my affairs, it almost drives me to distraction.

Saturday, May 26.—My brother Moses came to acquaint me of the death of Philip Turner, natural son of my half-sister, Elizabeth Turner (the boy we had the care of, as also his maintainance, according to the will of my father); he died this morn about five o'clock of a scarlet fever, aged fifteen years.

*

In the morn[1] I went over to Framfield, and, after taking an account of the gloves, hatbands, favours, &c., I set out for the funeral of Alice Stevens, otherwise Smith, natural daughter of Ben Stevens, at whose house she died. The young woman's age was twenty-eight years, and I think I never saw any person lament the death of any one more than Ben Stevens did for this poor girle, his daughter. As soon as it was possible we set out for Buxted Church, where she was to be buried with a large company of people, she being carried on men's shoulders; we arrived about twenty minutes past four, and where we heard an excellent sermon preached by the Rev. Mr. Lewson, curate of Buxted, froe the 27th verse, 9th chapter, Epist. Heb.—'And it is appointed unto men once to die, but after this the judgement.' The young woman was laid in the ground about fifty minutes past five.

[1] This entry belongs 'a few years' earlier, but Blencowe and Lower do not give a date. This exemplifies their practice of breaking the time sequence so as to bring related subjects together.

Tuesday, May 29.—In the afternoon, there was plaid at Hawkhurst Common, in this parish, a game of cricket, between this parish and that of Ringmer; but it was not plaid out, Ringmer having three wickets to go out, and thirty notches to get; so that in all probability, had it been plaid out, it would have been decided in favour of Hothly.

Fryday, June 1.—In the even, Mr. Banister and myself smoked a pipe[1] or two with Tho. Durrant, purely to keep Mr. Banister from quarrelling; his wife, big with child, lame of one hand, and very much in liquor, being out in the middle of the street, amongst a parcil of girls, boys, &c., Oh, an odious sight, and that more so to an husband!

Sunday, June 3.—We had a brief read for the rebuilding the parish church of Sittingbourn, in Kent, burnt down by the carelessness of workmen; the expence of rebuilding which, exclusive of the old materials and the parson's chancel, amounts to the sum of £2086, and upwards. The brief was to be gathered from house to house, in the several counties of Kent, Surry, and Sussex.

Fryday, June 8.—My old acquaintance Mr. Long (now an expectant in the excise) calld on me in the even, and took part of my bed.

Fryday, June 15.—I set out for Newhaven, where was to be a sale of foreign brandy at the customhouse. I dined at the White Hart, in company with five gentlemen (or, at least, other men). I then rosined

[1] See p. 11, note 1.

down my casks, and came home about twenty minutes to nine, very safe and sober.

Sunday, June 24.—In the morn, at thirty minutes past five, Tho. Durrant and I set out for Newhaven to see my very worthy friend Mr. Tipper,[1] where we arrived at fifty minutes past seven, and breakfasted with my friend Tipper; after which we entertained ourselves very agreably an hour or two. We also had the pleasure to see a lunet battery, erected there to guard the entrance of the harbour; it consists of five guns, 18-pounders, mounted, and everything ready for action. There is a very neat house and magazine belonging to the fort, and a gunner resident there. We dined with my friend Tipper, on a legg of lamb boiled, and fine white cabbage. We staid with my friend Tipper till thirty minutes past four, and then came away, and came home safe and well about three minutes past nine.

Saturday, June 30.—After breakfast, John French and I set out for Eastbourne; the reason of my journey was this:—Mrs. French's waggon, with her son and servant, was yesterday a-bringing a cord of wood to my house, and as they was before my door, came by Mr. Samuel Becket's postchaise and four horses, in the road from Uckfield to Eastbourne (their home), and in driving a great pace, with a sufficient

[1] Thomas Tipper, the famous Newhaven brewer of 'Newhaven Tipper' (strong beer); a man of great character and versatility. The full diary reveals him playing the violin, to Turner, and his memorial declares that 'He knew immortal Hudibras by heart.' B. and L.

degree of carelessness and audacity they in passing the fore horse of the team, drove against him, and, I presume by accident, drove the shaft of the chaise into the rectum of the horse, of which wound the horse died in about seven hours. Now, as I see the accident, Mr. French desired I would go with him to Mr. Beckett about it. We called at Mr. Fagg's on our journey, Mr. French wanting his advice, being a justice of the peace, who soon informed him, what he had been before told, that it was not justice busyness. Mr. Becket behaved extremely civil and agreable, and Mr. French, and he agreed to leave it to Mr. Fagg and Mr. Porter to appoint what he should pay for the damages, &c., sustained.

July 6.—This day came to Jones's a man with a cartload of milinery, mercery, linen-drapery, silver, &c., to keep a sale for two days,[1] which must undoubtedly be some hurt to trade; for the novelty of the thing (and novelty is surely the predominant passion of the English nation, and of Sussex in particular) will catch the ignorant multitude, and perhaps not them only, but people of sense, who are not judges of goods and trade, as indeed very few are; but, however, as it is it must pass.

July 11.—At home all day; busy in my garden all the forenoon; in the even I read part of Burnet's *History of the Reformation*, which I esteem a very impartial history, as the author has everywhere

[1] This type of licensed travelling vendor still makes seasonal visits to Sussex village halls.

treated his subject with moderation and coolness, which is, in my opinion, always a sign of learning and virtue.

Monday, July 30.—We had a tempest of thunder and lightning, and a great deal of rain; the storm here was not very severe, but it was excessive dark. I do not remember ever to have seen the heavens in so seeming a tempestuous a situation as they was to-day, the whole element seeming in a commotion. It did not last a great while.

Aug. 11.—Very unpleasant and irksome to myself to-day; the punch taken in to great a quantity last night, occasions my head to ach violently. A very fine pleasant day.

Monday, Aug. 13.—I spent the even till near ten o'clock in company with Joseph Fuller's family, Mr. Banister and Tho. Durrant, but I cannot say I came home sober. How do I lament my present irregular and very unpleasant way of life, for what I used to lead in my dear Peggy's time. I know not the comfort of an agreable friend and virtuous fair; no, I have not spent an agreable hour in the company of a woman since I lost my wife, for really there seem very few whoes education and way of thinking is agreable and suitable with my own.

Aug. 23.—Mr. Banister dined with me on some hashed venison, and after dinner we set out for Lewes races, where his Majesty's plate of £100 was run for on Lewes Downs, when Sir John Moore's grey horse, Cyclops, and Mr. Bowles' horse, Cyrus, started for it, which was won by Cyclops. I don't know I ever remember the King's plate being run in less time, they performing it in eight minutes and twenty-five seconds. Came home about three o'clock; but happy should I be if I could say sober. Oh, my unhappy, nay I may say, unfortunate disposition!—that am so irresolute, and cannot refrain from what my soul detests. See several London riders upon the downs, with whom I drank a glass or two of punch.

Saturday, Sept. 29.—My friend Mr. Elliss staid all night with me; I think my friend is as agreable a companion as any amongst my acquaintance, he being sober and virtuous, and a man of a great deal of good sense, and endued with good nature, and has improved his natural parts with a great deal of useful learning.

Thursday, Nov. 1.—I this day heard of the mellancholly news of the death of my old acquaintance and worthy friend, Mr. John Long, who died last night of the smallpox, under innoculation; a very sober and worthy young man, but from a bad constitution had the smallpox excessively full, and which proved mortal.

Sunday, Nov. 11.—During the time they was singing psalms, James Hudson, headborough,[1] and myself, went out and searched the alehouses and the

[1] A petty constable who served the Vestry under the Overseer, whom he periodically helped in matters of law and order (cf. 2 April 1758). He was also responsible for paying the village quota of County Militia Tax at Lewes Easter Sessions (in 1777 this was £10 18s.).

barber's shop; the barber we found exercising his trade,[1] but, as it was the first time, we forgave him. The alehouses was clear of tiplers. I think of all the company I ever spent the even with in my life, that of James Fuller is the most disagreable, he being stupidly ignorant, and withall prodigiously abusive.

Nov. 14.—This day was married, at our church, Mr. Simonds Blackman and Mary his wife (*alias* Mary Margenson). She being under age, some months agoe they went into Flanders, and was married at a place called Ypres; but as this marriage was not in all respects agreable to the laws of England, in regard to their issue enjoying the gentleman's estate, they was married this day by a licence, which styled her Mary Margison, otherwise Blackman. In my own private oppinion, I think, instead of making laws to restrain marriage, it would be more to the advantage of the nation to give encouragement to it; for by that means a great deal of debauchery would, in all probability, be prevented, and a greater increase of people might be the consequence, which, I presume, would be one real benefit to the nation—and I think it is the first command of the Parent and Governor of the universe, 'Increase and multiply,' and the observation of St. Paul is, that 'marriage is honourable in all men.'

Fryday, Nov. 23.—At home all day, and, thank GOD, very busy. Oh! how pleasant was the even

[1] Barbers were fined (2*s*. 6*d*. in Seaford in 1711) for shaving on Sunday. B. and L.

my journey to-day was this:—About four years ago, Mr. Porter bought of Mr. Burgess a farm; the house he has just now taken down; in doing of which, a bricklayer, in digging up the foundation, found several pieces, about four of old gold coin, of which one was a piece called a Jacobus, which I bought the 14th instant, for 20s., and some few pieces of silver, which I think is all that I have heard of been found. Now, Mr. Porter, as proprietor of the premises, and I doubt spurred on by self-interest (a vice very predominant in the breast of too many of us) claimed the same; but however, upon more mature deliberation and perswasion, has been brought over to think it belonged to the lord of the mannor, as un-doubtedly it does by the common law. It appears that about thirty-seven years agoe, the father of the present Mr. Burgess, who then lived in the house, was robb'd of several such old pieces of gold and silver, several gold rings, and about £5 in crown-pieces, none of which could never be found or heard anything of to this day, notwithstanding several people was at the time of the robery taken up on suspicion; therefore it is conjectured the money now found was, in all probability, a part of that which was taken; and it appears, from many circumstances, to be so. Mr. Burgess therefore applyed to a justice, to try if he could obtain any of this treasure trove; but alas! all in vain. As there could be no oath made to anything that has hitherto been found, no warrant could be granted; but Mr. Shelley, one of his

Majesty's justices of the peace, did grant a summons to have the man examined: a good-natured action, indeed, but what Mr. Justice had no business to grant; for I assure him it was common-law business, and his worship had no business with it. Mr. Burgess paid all expenses, and thankd me for my company, so I sped well enough. Sam. Jenner comming in the even, and being very much in liquor, staid all night.

Fryday, March 22.—I dined on some salt-fish, egg-sauce, parsnips, and potatoes. In the even read part of Homer's *Odyssey,* translated by Pope, which I like very well; the language being vastly good, and the turn of thought and expression beautiful.

March 28.—In the afternoon rode over to Chiddingly, to pay my charmer, or intended wife, or sweetheart, or whatever other name may be more proper, a visit at her father's, where I drank tea, in company with their family and Miss Ann Thatcher. I supped there on some rasures of bacon. It being an excessive wet and windy night I had the opportunity, sure I should say the pleasure, or perhaps some might say the unspeakable happiness, to sit up with Molly Hicks, or my charmer, all night. I came home at forty minutes past five in the morning—I must not say fatigued; no, no, that could not be; it could be only a little sleepy for want of rest. Well, to be sure, she is a most clever girl; but however, to be serious in the affair, I certainly esteem the girl, and think she appears worthy of my esteem.

Good Fryday.—In the even met with Molly Hicks,

by appointment, and walked home with her, where I staid with her, the weather being excessive bad, till past five in the morning, then came home.

Saturday, April 7.—In the even very dull and sleepy; this courting does not well agree with my constitution, and perhaps it may be only taking pains to create more pain.

Sunday, April 15.—After dinner I set out for Malling, to pay Molly Hicks, my intended wife, a visit, with whom I intended to go to church, but there was no afternoon service. I spent the afternoon with a great deal of pleasure, it being very fine, pleasant weather, and my companion very agreable. Now, perhaps, there may be many reports abroad in the world of my present intentions, some likely condemning my choice, others approving it; but as the world cannot judge the secret intentions of my mind, and I may therefore be censured, I will take the trouble to relate what really and truly are my intentions, and the only motive from which they spring (which may be some satisfaction to those who may happen to peruse my memoirs).[1] First, I think marriage is a state agreable to nature, reason, and religion; I think it the duty of every Christian to serve God and perform his religious services in the most calm, serene, and composed manner, which, if it can be performed more so in the married state than a single one, it must then be an indispensable duty. . . . . . As to my choice, I have only this to

[1] See p. 52, note 1.

say:—the girle, I believe, as far as I can discover, is a very industrious, sober woman and seemingly endued with prudence, and good nature, with a serious and sedate turn of mind. She comes of reputable parents, and may perhaps, one time or other, have some fortune. As to her person, I know it's plain (so is my own), but she is cleanly in her person, and dress, which I will say is something more than at first sight it may appear to be, towards happiness. She is, I think, a well-made woman. As to her education, I own it is not liberal; but she has good sense, and a desire to improve her mind, and has always behaved to me with the strictest honour and good manners—her behaviour being far from the affected formality of the prude, on the one hand; and on the other, of that foolish fondness to often found in the more light part of the sex. For myself, I have nothing else in view but to live in a more sober and regular manner, to perform my duty to GOD and man in a more suitable and religious manner, and, with the grace of the Supreme Being, to live happy in a sincere union with the partner of my bosom.

Wednesday, April 24.—A very pleasant even, and quite delightful; nothing wanting to make it so, except the company of my dear Molly and an easy mind.

Fryday, June 7.—In the even took a ride to pay my intended wife a visit, with whom I took a serious walk, and spent the even, till about ten o'clock. After parting with her, I went to take my horse, and, happening into company, I staid till ten minutes past twelve, and came home about four o'clock.[1]

Wednesday, July 3, 1765.—From the day last mentioned [*Sunday, June* 16], I have been so embarrassed with a multiplicity of business, that I was not able to continue my journal, being, on the 19th day of June, married, at our church, to Mary Hicks, servant to Luke Spence, Esq., of South Malling, by the Rev. Mr. Porter;[2] and for about fourteen days was very ill with a tertian ague, or, rather, an intermitting fever; then the ceremony of receiving visitors, and again the returning of them, has indeed, together with the business of my trade, taking up so much of my time, that I was obliged to omit that which would have given me the greatest pleasure imaginable to have continued; but, however, thank GOD, I begin once more to be a little settled, and am happy in my choice. I have, it's true, not married a learned lady, nor is she a gay one; but I trust she is good-natured, and one that will use her utmost endeavour to make me happy. As to her fortune, I shall one day have something considerable, and there seems to be rather a flowing stream. Well, here let us drop the subject, and begin a new one.

*

[1] He must have visited her in Lewes.

[2] Mr Porter was still remembered in 1859 by some of the aged inhabitants of East Hoathly, who say that he was much liked by his parishioners, being a kind-hearted man, and certainly of a convivial nature. B. and L.

The diary ends here. Thomas Turner died in 1793 at the age of sixty-three. The inscription on his gravestone in East Hoathly churchyard reads:

In
Memory of Thomas Turner of
This Parish Draper Who Died
February 6 1793 Aged 63 Years

Appendix

Notes on family history written by
THOMAS TURNER

The following autobiographical notes, formerly in the possession of my late father, Henry James Turner, have never previously been published.

They are contained in a small manuscript book bequeathed to Henry James Turner by his father, Charles Turner, who in turn had them from his father, Frederick Turner, son of the Diarist. That is the 'Frederick Turner, the third son of that name' whose birth is entered at the end of these notes as having occurred on Tuesday 17 December 1776.

F.M.T.

*

I Thomas Turner Son of John Turner by Elisabeth his second Wife was born at Groombridge in the parish of Speldhurst in the County of Kent on the Ninth day of June 1729 O.S.

My Father and his Family removed from Groombridge to Framfield in the County of Sussex on the 2nd day of June 1735 tho' he had been in possession of the Shop at Framfield from the 23 april 1735 O.S

I enter'd into Business for my self at East Hoathly in the County of Sussex at St. Michael 1750 O S

I had the misfortune (and to me a very great one) to loose my Father who died at Framfield on the 6 day of May 1752 O.S. and in the 63 year of his age, In him I lost the best of Parents, he was to me a Parent, Friend and Brother.

My Father left behind him a Widdow & 7 Children (to wit). By his First Wife Elisabeth Constable he had 1st John Turner born the 3 day of January 1716 O.S. and now in Business for himself at Tunbridge Wells whoes 1st Wife was Marg. Newman of the same place who lived with him about 17 Months & by whom he had one Daughter.

he remained a Widdow abt. 15 months and married his second Wife Mary Bennet who was his servt at the time of marriage, but her parents lived at Bidborrough in the County of Kent by whom he has many Children.

2d. Elisabeth Turner born 31 day of December 1718 O.S. (and who had a natural Son who my Father provided for by his last will) tho she unhappy wretch is now a Vagabond.

3d. William Turner born 22 day of March 1720 O.S. a servant to Mr. Richd Hill of Little Horsted

by his Widdow who was Eliz: Ovenden of Rotherfield in the County of Sussex 1st my self Born as before & in Business as before mentioned

2^{d}. Moses Turner Born the 29th day of June 1733 and then Apprentice to M^{r}. Isaac Hook, a Taylor in Lewis in the County of Sussex and whose apprenticeship expired on the 5 day of April 1754 N.S.

3^{d}. Sarah Turner Born the 17 Day of August 1738 O.S. then at School at Lewis.

4th. Richard Turner born the   Day of May 1742 O.S. at home when my Father died but since bound apprentice to M^{r}. Geo. Beard shopkeeper at Chailey to serve Seven Years from the 1st. day of January 1754 N.S. that being the day from which he was bound.

I was married at the parish Church of All-saints in Lewis, on Monday the 15th. day of October 1753 N.S To Margaret. Daughter of Sam: and Anne Slater of the parish of Hartfield in the County of Sussex and who at the time of Marriage Lived with M^{rs}. Pellet, at Lewis and who was born on the 29th. Day of November 1733 O.S. and By whom I had a Son born on Monday the 19th. day of August 1754 and who was Baptized on Tuesday the 3^{d}. Day of September by the name of Peter. His sponsors was M^{rs}. Roase & M^{r}. Tho. Scrase of Lewis & both in person & Joseph Fuller as proxy for M^{r}. John Madgwick of Lewis.

My Son Peter died at Framfield on Thursday the 16 day of Jan^{ry}. 1755 aged 21 weeks and 3 Days and was buried at Framfield on Saturday even following

April 1st. 1759

My Mother Elizabeth Turner Relict of my late Father John Turner died at Framfield on Sunday Morn the first day of April at about half an Hour paste Two O Clock in the Year 1759 and in the sixty-second year of her Age.

She was buried at Framfield on Thursday the 5th. of April at abt. 30 m p 8 in the Even.

My Beloved Wife Margaret Turner died in my dwelling house in East Hothly on Tuesday the 23d. day of June 1761 about Fifty-Minutes past One O Clock in the afternoon after a severe tho' lingering Illness which she had Labour'd under for upwards of 38 Weeks and which she bore with the greatest Patience & Resignation to the divine Will, she was aged 27 years 27 weeks & 6 days and was buried at Framfield on Saturday the Twenty Seventh day of June about 50 m p 6. In her I lost Everything that is Valluable in this World to me for she was un-doubtidly a Virtuous and Prudent Wife and One En-dued with a great many Qualifications therefore her death may be truly said to be an Inestimable loss to me & not to me only but the whole Neighbourhood in General

I Married June the 19th. 1765 Mary Daughter of Thomas and Mary Hickes of Chiddingly (then a Servant to Luke Spence Esqr. at South Malling) who was born January the 19th. (O.S.) 1735 By whom I had

Margaret Turner born the 20th. day of March 1766, Her Sponsors were M^{rs}. Atkins M^{rs}. French and M^{r}. Turner

Peter Turner Born the First day of June 1768 His Sponsors were my Broth^{r}. Moses, Sister Sarah, and M^{r}. Thomas Baldock

Philip Turner was Born October the 9th. 1769. His Sponsors were M^{r}. and M^{rs}. Smith and M^{r}. Walls.

Frederick Turner was Born December the 8th. 1771. His Sponsors were M^{r}. John Bredin, M^{r}. Edward Smith and M^{rs}. Porter [1]

Michael Turner was born the 29th. day of April 1773. His Sponsors were M^{r}. Snelling, M^{r}. Paine (both Surgeons) and M^{rs}. Walls.

My Brother Richard Turner died Monday the 21st. day of February 1774 at my House in East Hothly and was buried at Framfield Fryday the 25th. 1774 Aged 32 years

My little Boy Frederick died at my House after a few days Illness on Monday the 7th. day of November 1774 Aged two years and Ten Months and was buried at Framfield on Sunday the 13th. November.

[1] This lady was presumably the Rector's second wife.

Frederick Turner (the second Son of that name) was born on Wednesday the 3^d. day of May 1775. private baptized on Sunday the 14th. of May, inocculated for the Small Pox on tuesday the 30th. of may and died of that distemper on Tuesday Morn the 13th. day of June and was buried the same Evening privately in the Churchyard of Easthothly.

Frederick Turner the third Son of that name was born Tuesday the 17th. day of December 1776 and Baptized on Fryday the 10th. day of January 1777 his Sponsors were M^{rs}. Smith, (M^r. Smith as Proxy for his Son Frederick Smith) and M^r. Geoffery Taylor of Westerham.

Local Names

Checklist and Index of Thomas Turner's Contemporaries in East Hoathly and District

In a predominantly agricultural area many of the diarist's associates were farmers of some standing. Of the others in the diary, or relevant to it, some make but fleeting appearance, but sufficient to declare their trade or office. The occupations of almost all the rest have been deduced by reference to Turner's Overseer documents in the keeping of the Sussex Archaeological Society. I have omitted the names of many of those in the appendix as being of no great relevance to the diary.

G.H.J.

*Not mentioned in diary or appendix.

[1] See p. 69, note 1.

*Not mentioned in diary or appendix.

*Not mentioned in diary or appendix.

*Not mentioned in diary or appendix.

General Index

Compiled by
PATRICIA UTECHIN

GENERAL INDEX